THE ODYSSEY OF JOHN ANDERSON

In 1860 the American government made a formal request for the extradition of John Anderson, a fugitive slave living in Canada. At first glance the request was routine. But the legal, political, and diplomatic controversy that arose from this hearing threatened to topple the Canadian government, and aroused animosities between Britons and Americans.

John Anderson had been living quietly in Brantford, Canada West, when he was accused of killing a white man in Missouri in 1853. The American government, eager to placate the South on the eve of secession, demanded that Anderson be returned under the extradition treaty between the two countries.

Canadians were anxious to shield the fugitive from the almost certain lynching that awaited him in the South. During his court hearing in November 1860, a mob of outraged Torontonians surrounded the courthouse and threatened to release Anderson by force. Determined to maintain order, the authorities ordered police with fixed bayonets to protect the courts. This dissuaded the rescuers, and the matter was handled according to law. Nevertheless, the Cartier-Macdonald ministry was caught between the need to enforce the requirements of the law and the public outcry against extradition. In a display of political adroitness, John A. Macdonald saved both Anderson and the government.

At one point, a writ was issued from an English court to bring Anderson to London, and the prospect of a hunted fugitive appearing in an English courtroom reinvigorated the British anti-slavery movement. Americans from both the North and the South watched the Anderson case, and tried to gauge from it the British reaction to the emergence of the Confederacy. An obscure killing in Missouri became, for a brief period, an international cause célèbre.

Patrick Brode explores the legal and political implications of the Anderson case, and reveals something of the man at the centre of it all. John Anderson was an ordinary man caught in extraordinary circumstances. For a few months he was a public figure, a personification of the struggle against slavery. Not long after the hearing he dropped from public view, adding a final, unsolved mystery to this intriguing case.

PATRICK BRODE practises law in Windsor, Ontario. He is also a lecturer in the Faculty of Law, University of Windsor, and the author of *Sir John Beverley Robinson: Bone and Sinew of the Compact*.

John Anderson,
from a sketch probably made
while he was in England

The Odyssey
of John Anderson

PATRICK BRODE

Published for The Osgoode Society by
University of Toronto Press
Toronto Buffalo London

ISBN 0-8020-5840-x (cloth)
ISBN 0-8020-6748-4 (paper)

Printed on acid-free paper

Canadian Cataloguing in Publication Data

Brode, Patrick, 1950–
The odyssey of John Anderson

Includes bibliographical references and index.
ISBN 0-8020-5840-x (bound) ISBN 0-8020-6748-4 (pbk.)

1. Anderson, John, b. 1831? – Trials, litigation, etc.
2. Extradition – Canada. 3. Fugitive slaves – Canada
I. Osgoode Society. II. Title.

KE228.A53B76 1989   345.71'056'0924   C89-094264-1
KF223.A53B76 1989

Picture credits: all pictures are from the collection of the Law Society of Upper Canada except the frontispiece, John Anderson, from Harper Twelvetrees, ed. *The Story of the Life of John Anderson* (Freeport, NY 1971) and fugitive slaves, Public Archives of Canada PA123708.

Contents

PUBLICATIONS OF THE OSGOODE SOCIETY

For my mother and father

Foreword

THE OSGOODE SOCIETY

The purpose of The Osgoode Society is to encourage research and writing in the history of Canadian law. The Society, which was incorporated in 1979 and is registered as a charity, was founded at the initiative of the Honourable R. Roy McMurtry, at that time attorney general of Ontario, and officials of the Law Society of Upper Canada. Its efforts to stimulate legal history in Canada include the sponsorship of a fellowship, research support programs, and work in the field of oral history and legal archives. The Society publishes volumes that contribute to legal-historical scholarship in Canada and that are of interest to the Society's members. Included are studies of the courts, the judiciary, and the legal profession, biographies, collections of documents, studies in criminology and penology, accounts of great trials, and work in the social and economic history of the law.

The current directors of The Osgoode Society are Brian Bucknall, Mr Justice Archie Campbell, Douglas Ewart, Martin Friedland, Jane Banfield Haynes, John D. Honsberger, Kenneth Jarvis, Mr Justice Allen Linden, James Lisson, Brendan O'Brien, Peter Oliver, James Spence and Richard Tinsley. The attorney general for Ontario and the treasurer of the Law Society of Upper Canada are directors ex officio. The Society's honorary president is the Honourable R. Roy McMurtry. The annual report and information about membership may be obtained by writing The Osgoode Society, Osgoode Hall, 130 Queen Street West, Toronto, Ontario M5H 2N6. Members receive the annual volumes published by the Society.

Just before the outbreak of the American Civil War, a sensational case was heard in Toronto which captured headlines throughout North America and Europe. John Anderson, a fugitive slave who had been living quietly near Brantford, Ontario, was accused of having killed a white man in Missouri in 1853. The American government demanded that Anderson be extradited, and the ensuing legal proceedings created a storm of controversy in Canada.

The Odyssey of John Anderson is a compelling reconstruction of one of the most remarkable legal encounters in pre-Confederation Canada. Patrick Brode's account captures the drama of this exciting case and considers as well its larger political and legal implications. This book is an important contribution to the historical study of law and politics in Canada, and will be read with enjoyment and fascination by all.

Brendan O'Brien
President

Peter N. Oliver
Editor-in-Chief

Preface

Rarely has there been a case of such simplicity and purity in Canadian history as that of John Anderson. The plight of this black man who during his escape from slavery killed a white slave-owner brought out the deepest sympathies of the Canadian public. It was a case, as one of his supporters put it, 'of righteousness and holy law,' of a decent black man against a brutal 'slavocracy.' The case was suddenly and dramatically thrust before the public in November 1860. By March of the following year the controversy had faded away. Nevertheless, during its brief notoriety, this obscure incident in Missouri threatened to disrupt Anglo-American relations and even caused a rethinking of the rights of Canadians within the British empire.

Not only did the Anderson incident become a cause célèbre in Canada, it attracted the sympathies of the British and American anti-slavery movements. Abolitionists in three nations seized upon the case to show the world the bestial nature of slavery. Anderson's slave narrative was widely published in Europe and America. Yet such was the abolitionists' eagerness to profit from this incident that Anderson ceased to be a man and became instead a living symbol of oppression.

Although many Americans sympathized with the fugitive and feared that his extradition could destroy the underground railroad, others saw his case as a British provocation. The United States was already in upheaval: the Anderson hearings coincided with the secession of the southern states. In those anxious and often hysterical times, many

Americans regarded the British unwillingness to return an accused murderer as a deliberate insult. The Anderson case added to the bitter feelings between Britain and the United States which were to lead to the brink of war during the *Trent* affair.

The study of this one legal case is more than an exercise in the anecdotal. Through the Anderson case, Canadian society revealed the limits of its political and racial tolerance. In France, the study of specific legal cases is far more than mere histoire episodique. The political divisions between conservative and radical factions and the power of anti-Semitism were illustrated by the Dreyfuss affair. The trial of Henriette Caillaux in 1914 for the murder of her husband's defamer was an exposition of acceptable and unacceptable sexual conduct in French public life. Similarly, the Anderson case is an almost ideal study of Canadian attitudes towards the presence of fugitive slaves. The case revealed the passionate intensity of the movement (which had its origins in humanitarian and nationalistic urges) to defend the fugitives from American slavery. At the same time, the coolness and condescension with which John Anderson was treated showed the nation's tendency to keep the refugee blacks at a distance from white society.

During the brief notoriety of this case, the public avidly followed the proceedings in the Toronto courtrooms. The British public was especially transfixed by this distant drama, and when it appeared that a decision might be given against the fugitive, the British courts decided to intervene. This intervention represented the last attempt by a British court to issue a writ in Canada. The nationalistic resentment aroused by this imperial interference – and the insistence by Canadians that it be repudiated – was a measure of the sense of nationhood Canada had achieved by 1860.

Caught up in the emotion of the case, most Canadians chose to overlook these legal and international complexities. The question whether John Anderson was a murderer or a hero seemed moot. Pettifogging lawyers and diplomats might quibble about the case, but to the people Anderson personified the anti-slavery struggle. The popular perception that the courts were willing to send him back to the south to be burned to death by his enemies was a blow to the esteem of the judiciary. To the public, the issue was one of good versus evil; and they were unwilling to accept the judges' verdict to apply the written law to send this innocent man to his doom in the south.

Throughout this work the word 'Canada' applies only to the Province of

Canada – the English-speaking Upper Canada (Canada West) and the French-speaking Lower Canada (Canada East) as united by the Act of Union of 1840. When reference is made to other colonies, such as New Brunswick or Nova Scotia, the term 'British America' is used.

Like the Missouri slave-catchers, I have been on the trail of John Anderson for several years. I have had the help of the following persons and institutions: Mrs Kay Pettit of the State Historical Society of Missouri; Randy Roberts of the University of Missouri; William H. Cooper of the Ontario Archives; Wilma MacDonald of the Public Archives of Canada; and Carolyn A. Davis of the University of Syracuse. I am grateful for the help of the British Library and of Mr A. Lodge of the Rhodes House Library, Oxford. Special thanks are due to the staff of the Windsor Public Library for their unfailing help and courtesy.

The following individuals assisted and encouraged this effort: Bryan Walls, Howard McCurdy, MP, Dale Richardson, Vivian Robinson, Dr Larry Kulisek, and Dr Ian Pemberton. I am also grateful for the counsel and help of Dr Peter Oliver, Dr John Benyon, and Rebecca Livingston of the U.S. National Archives. I would especially like to thank Kathy Johnson, whose fine editorial hand has graced this book.

I would like to thank the Canada Council for its encouragement and its generous support of this research.

Matthew Crooks Cameron,
one of John Anderson's defenders
and later an Ontario judge

Sir John Beverley Robinson.
The Anderson case was to be his
last major hearing.

Robert A. Harrison,
Crown prosecutor.
Shown in later life as chief justice of Ontario

Court of Queen's Bench.
The courtroom, still in use,
is in Osgoode Hall.

Archibald McLean,
justice of Queen's Bench,
and fervid abolitionist

Fugitive slaves in Canada West
in the 1850s

The Odyssey of John Anderson

1

In Little Dixie

The odyssey began in Africa. John Anderson's forefathers were brought to America in bondage to work the plantations of the southern states. As ambitious settlers moved west, their slaves travelled with them. John Anderson's mother was owned by Moses Burton, a tobacco farmer and tradesman in Howard County, Missouri. At the time of John's birth, around 1831, Burton had achieved prosperity and was the owner of several slaves.

A fierce rebellious streak characterized John's parents. His father, described as 'almost white,' was a steward on a Missouri River steamer. Shortly after John's birth he escaped from slavery, and it was rumoured that he sailed to South America. John remembered his mother as 'a great big spirit, something like me, and wouldn't stand being beat about and knocked around.' One day, when John was about seven, she came to blows with her mistress and succeeded in pulling a handful of hair out of Mrs Burton's head. She was forthwith sold down the Mississippi River to a Louisiana plantation.[1] It is ironic that the sturdy independent settlers, such as the Burtons, who characterized America's westward expansion should have been so intolerant of any sign of independence on the part of their human chattels.

Even though Missouri possessed vast natural wealth, its early years were marked by violence. During the 1830s a vicious religious war had resulted in the Mormons' being driven from the state. Yet it was the slavery issue that was to dominate political passions and cause extensive violence and bloodshed.

Missouri's early settlers were attracted by the deep, fertile soil of the central part of the state. Most came from the southern states, and as a matter of course they brought their black slaves with them. These settlers formed a 'Little Dixie' in Howard, Boone, and Callaway counties. By 1860 it was reported that Little Dixie contained areas in which there was one slave for each white inhabitant.[2] Yet even though the number of Missouri bondsmen had increased from 9,797 in 1820 to 114,931 in 1860, slaves were a declining percentage of the total population. Missouri was attracting tens of thousands of white settlers who farmed without slaves. But popular sentiment in favour of chattel bondage was so strong that only a few brave men spoke out for emancipation: 'From statehood to 1860, most Missourians vigorously defended slavery even though a small percentage of them actually owned slaves.'[3]

Slavery in Missouri reflected the prevailing attitudes towards blacks both as chattels and as members of an inherently inferior race. By law slaves were not permitted to learn how to read or write, to hold their own religious services, or to be legally married.[4] A slave could not own property or testify at the trial of a white person. The law discouraged the escape of slaves by permitting any white man to detain a black he suspected of being a runaway.

But a slave's life was not necessarily a cycle of brutality and humiliation. It has been suggested that what the planters wanted was 'devoted, hard-working, responsible slaves who identified their fortunes with the fortunes of their masters.'[5] It appears that for his first twenty years in bondage, John Anderson was content with his lot. At this point in his life Anderson was known by his master's name, and was called 'Jack Burton.' Once in Canada, he would assume a variety of names, including 'William Jones' and 'William Anderson.' 'John Anderson' was the name he used regularly, however, and the name in which legal proceedings were conducted. After his own mother was sold, Anderson was raised by Mrs Burton; even after he had gained freedom he referred to her affectionately as his mother. Jack was raised in the household as a playmate and a 'kind of nurse' to the Burtons' two daughters. When he was fourteen or fifteen he was sent to the field to work. Shortly thereafter he was put in charge of the tobacco crop and made supervisor of the other slaves. 'I had to see the work done,' he recalled, 'and had to knock the other slaves about to make them do it.' Moses Burton even gave young Jack one and a half acres of land so that he could raise and sell his own crops.[6]

In 1850 Anderson began to court Maria Tomlin, the daughter of Lewis Tomlin, a freed slave. Lewis had saved enough money to buy himself and his wife from his master, Samuel Brown, and was operating a barber shop in the town of Fayette. A slave had to be unusually shrewd to purchase his own freedom; even then, the legal restrictions on freed slaves left them at the mercy of their white neighbours.[7] Maria Tomlin had been born while her father was still in bondage, so she remained the property of Samuel Brown. She had entered into a slave marriage in her youth and had borne two children when her husband died. It was at her husband's funeral that Jack first saw and became infatuated with Maria. About six months after the funeral he arranged to take her to a religious camp meeting. For the slaves the camp meetings were an excuse for social and recreational as well as religious revivals. A sober adherent of the Free Will Baptists, Anderson observed with some dismay that 'many slaves, who have no religion, go to camp meetings that they may be merry, for there is much whisky sold at these gatherings, and the people drink and play at cards, while other attend to religion.' It appears that Anderson paid at least as much attention to Maria as he did to his spiritual obligations. He was rebuffed by Lewis Tomlin, however, and told to be more restrained in the courting of his widowed daughter. Impatiently, Jack confided to Maria that if her father did not consent to their marriage, 'we'll be married all the same.' In the face of this determination Lewis relented, and Jack and Maria were wed according to slave tradition. Maria made her husband promise to devote himself to buying her freedom and that of her children. Jack was much in love with Maria, and was obsessed with trying to gain for his family the freedom enjoyed by his father-in-law.

All of his expectations were destroyed in the summer of 1853. Burton had permitted Anderson to visit the Brown farm to see Maria only on weekends. But he had grown increasingly impatient with the restrictions of slave life. It became Anderson's habit to visit his wife and his newborn child every evening, and sometimes to stay until morning. Moses Burton had come to resent Anderson's disregard for his authority. He accosted him one morning upon his return: 'Jackey, where have you been?' Anderson replied, 'Oh, I've been walking about.' 'I'll walk you about!' the infuriated Burton shouted. He tried ineffectually to whip Anderson with a rawhide. He then threw a rope over the branch of a tree and ordered Anderson to strip and prepare for a flogging. Anderson refused, and, in a rage, Burton returned with a gun and threatened to shoot him on the spot. Only the intervention of Burton's daughters, Jack's former play-mates, prevented the planter from carrying out his intention. For the moment, Burton's anger cooled. 'He then said he only wanted to frighten me, but that he would sell me to someone who would break my spirit.'[8]

Jack had always been Mrs Burton's favourite, and after her death, he felt, 'Burton made up his mind to conquer me.' A clash between master and slave was inevitable.

By this time, Jack had gained a reputation among the local planters as a troublesome slave, as being 'savage and ill-disposed.' The outstanding complaint against him seemed to be his unwillingness to submit to punishment. Shortly after his confrontation with Burton, he was again ordered to go to the barn and receive a flogging. This time Burton's daughters took their father's side, and urged Jack to submit. Once again he refused. Nothing further occurred, but Anderson was surprised when much of the tobacco harvesting was left to others. In August 1853 Burton told Jack that he had been sold to Colonel Reuben Ellis McDaniel of Saline County. On the day he was sold, Anderson witnessed the transaction and saw McDaniel hand over one thousand dollars to Burton. Surprised at the price, Anderson immediately turned on Burton: 'That's a great deal of money, and I think you ought to give me some of it.' Burton made no response. The troublesome slave who had the gall to demand a share of his own sale price had now become some other master's problem.

Taking charge of his new chattel, McDaniel travelled westward to the Missouri River. Together, master and slave crossed the river. When they landed on the western shore, Anderson overheard McDaniel lean over and tell the ferryman 'to take care he never allowed me to recross it.' During the buggy ride to the plantation, McDaniel gave his new slave a lecture on escaping: any attempt to flee would earn Anderson a good flogging, and would result in his being sold to the New Orleans slavers.

Anderson was about to experience the harsher and more common face of slavery. It is probably true that 'cruelty was endemic in all slaveholding communities,'[9] and life on the McDaniel plantation showed the corrosive consequences of slavery for owners as well as for their slaves. The first thing Anderson noticed upon his arrival was the hungry, miserable look of the other blacks. His slave-driver was told to work the new slave 'into the traces by degrees.' Worst of all, for Anderson, was his separation from Maria. After a few weeks he asked for permission to go to Fayette to see his wife and bring back some clothes. McDaniel made it plain that Anderson would never be permitted to see Maria again, and that he might as well choose one of the slave girls for companionship. Life as one of McDaniel's breeding stock was, to a man of Anderson's spirit, unthinkable.

He resolved to leave Missouri and seek a reunion with Maria whenever he could. Among the slaves word had spread of a place where they could be free, with no fear of bounty-hunters who would return them to the slave states. An old slave named Jacob had told John 'about Canada, and I had talked with other slaves about starting off for that place.'[10] Anderson chose a Sunday near the end of September for his escape. Sunday was a day of rest on the farm, and McDaniel had been called to his church to discuss the case of a fellow planter who had whipped a slave to death. Without raising any alarm, Anderson took a mule and a length of rope, and headed towards the Missouri River.

After a day of travelling he reached Fayette, and told his father-in-law of his plans. Lewis Tomlin agreed that his only choice now was to run from slavery, and offered him a pistol. Anderson declined, and said that he had a dirk knife that should be satisfactory. He then visited the Brown farm to say goodbye to Maria and their child. That night he began the odyssey which he hoped would lead to freedom.

2

A Sudden Impulse

The summer of 1853 had been a hot, anxious time in Little Dixie. Newspapers warned their readers of 'Negro outrages,' of 'stampedes' of Negroes heading for the free states. Missouri was an embattled bastion of slavery trying to maintain an imperilled institution. Under the headline 'Abolition Rascality' the *Boonville Observer* reported the machinations of a daring Canadian abolitionist, F.H. Moss. Working with a freed slave, Moss had infiltrated slave quarters around Boonville and persuaded a number of bondsmen to run off to Canada. The newspaper hoped that the revelation of this plot would 'place the public on their guard as to the organized efforts of incendiaries.'[1]

Even more shocking were reports of slave attacks against whites. 'A Negro man, entirely naked, rushed from a thicket, close by, and attempted to violate her person,' reported a Howard County newspaper in 1853.[2] The young lady's resistance prevented the assailant from 'accomplishing his designs.' Shortly after this incident a slave named Hiram was charged with attempted rape. His owner hired legal counsel for him; before his trial was complete, however, he was seized by a ferocious mob and hanged. While agreeing that this was a justified punishment, the *Liberty Tribune* warned that 'the forcible seizure and execution of a prisoner under trial is a dangerous doctrine.'[3] A more horrific incident occurred in nearby Pettis County. After raping and murdering a pregnant white woman, a slave was seized by a mob and burnt at the stake. This horrible punishment was the result of 'frequent attempts of late years, of negroes to rape white women ... and the impression among the community that it required such an example to protect them from the repetition of similar outrages.'[4] Mob justice was common in Missouri in 1853, and the mere accusation of murder against a man of any colour could well result in a swift hanging. In October 1853 a white man was arrested on a murder charge in Ray County. Before his trial could take place, a mob stormed the jail and lynched him. A local newspaper casually observed that 'mob law is gaining ground in our State.'[5]

The white population of Little Dixie was becoming increasingly uneasy about the possibility of a slave rebellion. They were already concerned about the economic loss caused by runaway slaves. According to one report, over a thousand runaways had passed into Canada in 1853, resulting in a loss to their owners of $2 million.[6] The state legislature had acted to curb this loss of human capital by passing laws enabling any white Missourian to seize runaways. A reward of five dollars was paid for this service.[7]

Seneca Digges, a farmer who held land north of Fayette, was well aware of these provisions. It was an economic fact of life that all owners should co-operate to prevent runaways from escaping. Digges owned a number of slaves, and was vigilant in apprehending escaped slaves from fellow planters. A tall, slightly built man, Seneca Digges was well respected in the community. Because his health was poor, he left all the hard work on his farm to his slaves. On Tuesday, 28 September 1853, Digges, in the company of four of his slaves and his young son Ben, was returning to the farmhouse for the noon meal. He was about to have a chance meeting with John Anderson, a meeting that would have tragic consequences for both men.

Anderson was into his third day of escape. Unwisely, he was travelling during the daytime and was sure to be spotted. When he encountered Digges, he could not avoid answering the inevitable question about his pass. Anderson replied that he belonged to McDaniel of Saline County, but that he had permission to visit the farm of Charles Givens to try and persuade Givens to buy him so that he could remain near his wife. Digges was immediately suspicious, for he knew that no slave could have travelled thirty miles from his master without a pass. Anderson was told to fall in with the other slaves and have dinner with them. He went along quietly, and was walking with the other slaves when suddenly he turned and bolted for the nearby woods.

Seven years later a Canadian magistrate in Brantford would try to piece together what had happened that Tuesday afternoon.[8] Various witnesses would come forward, including Ben Digges, who had been eight years old when his father died. Ironically, the only witness who was able to identify Anderson and name him as the assailant was a fellow black, Digges's slave Phil. In *Rashomon*-like fashion, even the victim, Seneca Digges, would return to render his account.

As Anderson fled, Digges ordered his slaves to chase him, and called out that whoever captured the runaway could keep the reward money. After about half an hour of pursuit, the four blacks caught up to Anderson and began to encircle him. Seeing that he was surrounded, Anderson pulled out his dirk knife. According to Phil, he called out that 'he would kill us if we came near him.' Breaking out of the encirclement, Anderson ran across a wood pasture and was just approaching a fence when he ran straight into Seneca Digges. Digges and his son had been following the chase at a distance when Anderson suddenly appeared before them. Ben recalled that his father had just crossed the fence when '[he] was first stabbed in the breast. After that father turned to run away and hung his foot in some vines and fell. The man then stabbed him in the back, and then broke and run.' The planter had struck out at Anderson with a paw-paw stick, but the stick broke and did not stop the blow.

Before his death Digges told his eldest son Thomas that 'the negro ran at him and stabbed him … The negro cut him a little in the wrist; he then stabbed him in his breast.' Thomas Digges also swore that his father told him that he was trying to get away when he was stabbed again. 'He turned to leave and his feet caught in something, and while he was in the act of falling, or had fallen, he stabbed him again in the back.' The stories of Digges's sons were consistent. The hapless planter was confronted by a desperate, armed runaway, and was himself trying to escape when he received his third stab wound. This kind of detail is absent from the sworn deposition of the slave Phil. He recalled that 'at last master met the negro, and I saw him cut master twice with a knife. I saw him when he run at my master with the knife.' But there is no indication of how close Phil was when he saw the stabbing. Surprisingly, Phil and the other slaves continued to pursue Anderson and gave no assistance to their fallen master.

Later versions of the attack, as published by abolitionists, would add a good deal of provocation to Digges's conduct. According to these reports, Digges threw an axe at Anderson and ordered his slaves to take the runaway dead or alive. Digges and his minions became armed with 'clubs,' and it was necessary for Anderson to strike the planter twice 'to prevent pursuit ... and effectually disarm him.'[9] The sworn depositions given to the magistrate at Brantford are probably closer to the truth. Anderson heard these depositions, and in his own petition he conceded that his knowledge of the facts was 'in nearly the manner mentioned in the [Crown's] evidence.'[10] According to Anderson, he had almost eluded the pursuers, 'and at the moment he was looking for success Mr Digges appeared before him.' In the next instant the fugitive knew he had no alternative, 'and being borne on with the first impulse he dashed against said Digges with an open knife with which he had threatened his pursuers.' Whether he had struck the planter once or twice was a detail he could no longer recall.

Anderson was probably exhausted and desperate at the time he stabbed Digges. He had been a fugitive for three days and was on the verge of being run down and captured. Capture for him meant, at best, a severe flogging. At worst he could expect to be branded or maimed and then sold to a Louisiana plantation to spend the remainder of his life at back-breaking labour. As he later explained, 'Whatever sudden impulse bid, that he did, to obtain his liberty.'[11]

Although he must have known that gangs of vigilantes would soon be after him, Anderson retraced his path to Fayette. He had to see his wife one last time and tell her what had happened. When he told Maria of the stabbing, she insisted that he leave immediately. The word had already gone around the slave quarters that 'some old slaveholder [had] been struck by a Negro with a knife.'[12] It was now doubly important that Anderson get out of Missouri as quickly as possible. If he was captured now, he would undoubtedly face a quick and merciless punishment. After one more farewell, he left Fayette.

He was never to see Maria again.

Little Benjamin Digges knelt over his father and wondered what he should do next. After about an hour he heard some of the family's slaves nearby, and called for them to come. The slaves appeared in the company of Dr Samuel Crewse, one of Digges's neighbours. Blankets were fetched, and the injured planter was taken to Dr Crewse's house. Seneca Digges was in great pain, and seemed aware that he could never recover from so serious a wound. He spoke to his son Thomas and to a neighbour, William C. Baker, and told them what had occurred. Two weeks after the incident, on 11 October 1853, Digges died of the stab wounds.

Howard County was in an uproar. A reward was offered for Anderson's capture, and a 'large party of gentlemen' started in pursuit of him.[13]

A few days after the stabbing a mass meeting of Howard County residents was convened at the court house in Fayette. The purpose of the meeting was to devise 'means to suppress insubordination among slaves.' A committee of vigilance was appointed for each township 'whose duty it shall be to observe the conduct of persons suspected of intermeddling with the slave population.' It was resolved by the committee that the 'repeated outrages committed by the negroe population' were probably formented by 'evil disposed white persons' (such as the Canadian abolitionist F.M. Moss), and that vigilance was essential to stop this sedition.[14]

Vigilantes and professional bounty-hunters were soon hot on Anderson's trail. One bounty-hunter caught him resting at the side of the road, but Anderson managed to slip away into a field of tall corn. Later that same evening Anderson saw a fire on a hill and thought it might have been felow slaves husking corn. When he approached the hill, it turned out to be an ambush arranged by the same bounty-hunter, and Anderson barely escaped.[15] Local newspapers reported that 'the negro was seen in Monroe county, hotly pursued and fired upon,'[16] but that he had eluded the vigilantes.

Travelling only at night, Anderson was desperate to cross the Mississippi River and get to a free state. He stole what food he could, and usually had to eat it raw for fear that a fire would attract the slave-catchers. Two weeks after leaving McDaniel's farm he reached the Mississippi. He crossed the river in a stolen boat, and reached the free state of Illinois. Even in free territory he was not safe. He was still liable to be returned to Missouri as a fugitive slave, and now as a murderer. But Illinois contained many abolitionists who would be willing to help him. On one occasion an English settler gave Anderson a meal and a bed for the night.

As he passed through the Illinois countryside, his clothes became so ragged and torn that 'the children [came] running to the doors to stare at him.' There was no time to stop, for he remained terrified of being recaptured. At one farmhouse he paused to purchase a loaf of bread for ten cents. Upon hearing a man enter the house, Anderson rushed out the door and down the lane. He was followed by the farm wife, who angrily demanded her money. After he calmed down, Anderson paid her for the bread and went on his way.

Eventually, he reached Chicago. Local abolitionists provided him with lodgings: he lived with a barber for three weeks until the abolitionist society paid for him to travel east to Detroit, and from there across the river to Windsor, Canada West. Upon his arrival in Windsor in November 1853, Anderson was, at last, genuinely a free man. No slave catchers could legally return him to Missouri, and in any event he had long since shaken off his pursuers.

After arriving in Canada, Anderson worked for a few weeks as a labourer on the Great Western Railway. With his earnings he bought new clothes and enrolled himself in a school for fugitive slaves. This school was run by the remarkable Henry Bibb, himself an escaped slave from Kentucky. Bibb also had founded and edited a newspaper, the *Voice of the Fugitive*, and established the Fugitive Home Society.[17] It was a sign of Anderson's determination to improve himself that he resolved to work only part time so that he could attend Henry Bibb's school.

John Anderson was free, but he had not outrun the memories of his home. Laura Haviland, a teacher at the Bibb School, was struck by his 'settled sadness.' One day she accompanied him back to his boarding-house, and he told her of his escape and his desolation at being separated from his wife and child. At the end of his story Anderson 'buried his face in his handkerchief, [and] his whole athletic frame became convulsed with grief.' Laura Haviland was so struck by his plight that she resolved somehow to reunite Anderson with his wife. She wrote to Lewis Tomlin; for safety's sake, she posted the letter from a Michigan address.[18] In April 1854 Anderson received some astounding news. Mrs Tomlin had died, and Lewis was going to travel north with Maria, who would pose as his wife. Anderson was overjoyed, but Laura Haviland cautioned him that it might be a ruse. His yearning for his wife was understandable; none the less, he should have suspected that the authorities in Howard County were watching the Tomlins for any clue to his whereabouts.

Neither Anderson nor Mrs Haviland could know of the events that were taking place back in Missouri. Poor old Lewis Tomlin had been convicted of harbouring Anderson. He had received five lashes, and had been ordered to leave the state forthwith.[19] Anderson's letter to Lewis was read by the Howard County police, and the trail that had grown so cold was fresh again. A Missouri bounty-hunter named Brown was sent to Michigan to bring the fugitive back to the state. Brown was an efficient, ruthless hunter. If he could only locate Anderson, it would be a simple matter to arrest and extradite him. Brown hired local detectives, a Mr Warren of Detroit and Samuel Port of Windsor, to assist him in the capture.

A wary Laura Haviland crossed the border to meet with Warren and a white southerner who claimed to have conducted the Tomlins to Detroit.

Mrs Haviland carefully questioned the southerner, and satisfied herself that 'he was a bogus coin.' She told him that Anderson had escaped to Canada and would never re-enter the United States. With the knowledge that the bounty-hunters were back on his trail, Anderson headed towards the town of Chatham.

Chatham lay fifty miles east of Windsor and fifty miles farther from the American border. There was a substantial fugitive population in the town, and Anderson hoped that by changing his name and mixing with the other fugitives he could avoid detection. He had been in the town for several days when the other fugitives warned him that white strangers were asking after a Missouri runaway named Jack. A group of fugitives cornered the bounty-hunter Brown and threatened to turn the tables and lynch him. One slave-catcher had been caught in Windsor, and had been nearly whipped to death by the friends of the slave he was pursuing.[20] Brown was aware of his danger, and by drawing his weapons managed to keep the revenge-minded blacks at bay until he was rescued by the local police.[21] In the meantime Anderson changed his name again and headed farther east. Brown had lost the trail, and, mindful of his narrow escape, gave up the chase.

Laura Haviland later recalled that the governor of Missouri, with the authority of the secretary of state, had requested Anderson's extradition. She in turn wrote to the governor general of Canada, Lord Elgin, urging him that if Anderson was to be tried, the trial should be before a British court.[22] But John Anderson was nowhere to be found.

Nothing further was heard of John Anderson for six years, but the South had not forgotten him. In 1856 Laura Haviland carried on a lively debate about slavery with a New Orleans attorney. At one point she described a hypothetical case with Anderson in mind. The southerner interrupted her, saying that he knew she was referring to the case of John Anderson, and that 'we shall have Anderson and make an *example* of him.' He promised Haviland and her abolitionist friends that one day the South would capture John Anderson: 'We are going to have Anderson by hook or by crook; we will have him by fair means or foul; the South is determined to have that man.'[23]

3

Magistrate Mathews's Prisoner

Canada West, John Anderson's haven from slavery and lynching, fell well short of being an egalitarian society. As Henry Bibb editorialized, 'wicked and cruel prejudice' existed, 'even in Canada.'[1] Slavery had existed in Canada West from the first days of the province until the 1790s, when laws were passed that restricted the institution. By the 1820s slavery had all but died out. The Imperial Act of 1833 finally abolished slavery throughout the British empire.

Small numbers of blacks had inhabited the province since its founding by loyalists at the close of the American Revolution. One black loyalist, Richard Pierpoint, served in the British forces in both the Revolutionary War and the War of 1812.[2] By the 1830s the proportion of blacks living in this westernmost province of British America was still relatively small. For the most part the blacks were respectable citizens. William Lyon Mackenzie, the firebrand who ignited the Rebellion of 1837, once complained that the black settlers were 'extravagantly loyal.'[3] During the rebellion nearly one thousand black Canadians volunteered for military service in the first month. The 'coloured companies' performed well, although on one occasion a company learned of two female slaves who were being held on Canadian soil and, without authority, promptly liberated them.[4]

Especially after the passage of the Fugitive Slave Act in 1850, desperate blacks were forced to go to British America for refuge. This influx of runaways, as well as of free blacks who were fearful of re-enslavement, was substantial. Although no reliable figures exist, the increase in the black population was significant enough to cause a violent white reaction. Efforts to establish a refugee settlement in Elgin County were met by a petition from the residents stating that a 'Colony of ... Vicious Blacks' was not wanted. White residents of Chatham petitioned the government to stop all further black immigration. In 1857 Colonel John Prince articulated the widely held belief that the refugees were mostly shiftless thieves. Prince declared that the blacks in Essex County had been treated with 'invariable kindness,' which had been repaid with 'robbing, pilfering and plunder.'[5] If Canada West had to accept the fugitives, he suggested that they be confined to remote Manitoulin Island. Clearly, hostility to the refugee blacks was growing.

Even those abolitionists who wanted to help the fugitives usually tempered their charity with condescension. Many of the escaped slaves ended up in the missionary settlements of Dawn and Wilberforce, which reinforced the prevailing wisdom that blacks were unable to manage their affairs without white direction. This paternalism was condemned by Frederick Douglass, who, in a Toronto speech in 1851, urged his Canadian brothers to make their own way as independent citizens, to use 'self-exertion and self-cultivation ... in order to place [themselves] on an equality with white men.' Equality would be hard to realize in a society in which blacks were regarded by most as inferior and by some as dangerous nuisances. There was a widely held but unsubstantiated view among whites that blacks occupied Canadian jails and asylums in disproportionate numbers. Blacks were regularly denied employment, opportunities to buy houses, and admission to hotels. 'British North Americans shared the patterns of prejudice found in the North, although these patterns appeared in colors muted by distance from the central scene of action.'[6]

Perhaps indicative of white Canadian attitudes towards blacks were the comments of the province's chief justice, Sir John Beverley Robinson. He was the descendant of Virginia loyalists, a family of slave-owners who keenly resented the government's attempts in the 1790s to put an end to slavery. On one occasion Robinson reported the case of a black man who had been convicted of cattle theft and had then fled the province. 'I think I would have him where he is,' Robinson warned. 'They have too many such people about Amherstburg already.'[7] Robinson's low opinion of blacks was counterbalanced by his determination that all men would be treated fairly under the law. Earlier in his career, when he was the attorney general, Robinson had been asked whether slaves were 'self-stolen' property and liable to be returned to their owners. He replied in the negative: 'Freedom of the person being the most important civil right protected by those [British] laws, it follows that whatever may have been the condition of these Negroes in the country to which they formerly belonged – here they are free.'[8] As a result of Robinson's opinion, no slave could be returned to his master merely because he had sought freedom in Canada.

Robinson's legal opinion illustrated the inconsistency of Canadian attitudes to the fugitive slaves. On the one hand they were considered to be inferior and to be kept apart. On the other hand they were equal in the eyes of the law, and British justice was to be applied irrespective of colour. Blacks served on juries, voted, and were taxed the same as their white fellow subjects. One black man, Abraham Shadd, was elected to a town council in 1859. It may be true that equality in law helped to temper the discrimination that existed in fact. Although the province has been criticized for the intolerant attitude of many of its citizens,[9] it is possible that this criticism is exaggerated. After all, Canada did provide a haven from slavery, a place where fugitives such as Anderson could live as free men, equal under the law. One escaped slave, John H. Hill, expressed a view that was probably common among the fugitives: 'I wants you to let the whole United States know we are satisfied here because I have seen more Pleasure since I came here than I saw in the U.S. the 24 years that I served my master.' On another occasion he added, '[Canada] is the best poor man's country that I know of.'[10] Indeed, that John Anderson learned a trade and bought property is proof that for many of the escaped slaves Canada was the promised Canaan.

On one point most British Americans were agreed. While they might dislike the fugitive slaves in their midst, they were proud that those unfortunates could find liberty in the province. It was a continual source of self-congratulation that no man was in bondage in British America, while in the supposedly free United States millions were enslaved. Many wished to stop the black influx, but some heartily supported the refugees. In 1851 the Anti-Slavery Society of Canada was established. Prominent on the executive committee were George Brown, the powerful editor of the Globe, and a young lawyer, Oliver Mowat, later to be the province's premier. The society became an active political body, agitating against slavery and supporting the abolitionist movement in the United States.[11]

A fugitive slave's greatest fear was that he might face criminal extradition, for it was virtually impossible to escape from slavery without committing some offence. One might have to steal a horse or forge a master's name on a pass. To what extent did this render a fugitive slave liable to extradition?

Complicating this issue was the fact that ordinary criminals crossed and recrossed the long, unguarded border between the United States and British America as a means of evading justice. To put an end to this temptation, the province passed the Fugitive Offenders' Act in 1833.[12] This act gave the lieutenant-governor the authority to extradite persons accused of murder, forgery, larceny, or felonious crimes. Significantly, the return of these offenders was to be made only 'at [the lieutenant-governor's] discretion.' There did not exist any legal obligation to return an accused. Extradition was therefore an administrative and political procedure as well as a legal one.

The difficulty for the authorities (and more so for the fugitives) was that slaveowners might attempt to regain their chattels by charging them with criminal offences committed during their escape. Two cases illustrate the difficulty faced by Canadian officials in expelling criminals and preserving British America as a haven for fugitive slaves.

In 1833 Jesse Happy had taken his master's horse to effect his escape from Kentucky. With consummate thoughtfulness he left the horse on the American side of the border and wrote to his master, telling him how to find it. Public sympathy lay with Happy, but the extradition laws had to be enforced. The colonial government sought Chief Justice Robinson's advice: he replied that the return of felons to the place of the crime was the most important consideration. Moreover, 'to proclaim impunity to all slaves who may fly to Upper Canada after murdering or robbing their Masters, or others would be inviting a description of population which, to say the least, it is not desirable to encourage.'[13]

The province's lieutenant-governor, Sir Francis Bond Head, was reluctant to return Happy. He felt that Happy's former owner was probably the 'blackest criminal of the two.' The provincial authorities handled this problem as they did most difficult questions – the matter was referred to London. On the one hand, the Crown law officers agreed with the Canadians that there was insufficient evidence of horse-theft. Happy had not intended to deprive his master of his property, and therefore he should not be extradited. On the other hand, they felt that when there was evidence of criminality the accused 'ought to be delivered up, without reference to the Question of whether he is, or is not, a Slave.' Canada West as a refuge from slavery no longer looked so secure.

The Crown law officers added, as an afterthought, that a surrender should be made only if there was evidence of criminality as 'would warrant the apprehension of the accused Party, if the alleged offence had been committed in Canada.'[14] That is, 'double criminality' must exist. The offence had to be a crime in the state holding the prisoner as well as in the state requesting extradition. From this routine comment a myth has arisen that there existed an implied 'anti-slavery principle,' that 'since slavery did not exist in Canada, any act which a slave committed as part of his escape could be considered in the context of self-defence.'[15] According to this view there was no need to exempt fugitive slaves from the laws of extradition, for the concept of 'double criminality' protected them: 'Through experience the British government learned that it was not necessary to submit to the abolitionist demand that fugitive slaves be specifically exempted from normal extradition procedures; sufficient protection for them was found in adherence to certain traditional legal rules reinforced by an ever-present sympathy for these refugees from American slavery.'[16] 'Double criminality' was not a new rule; the Swiss jurist Vattel referred to it in 1758 in *The Law of Nations.* Extradition would result from 'great crimes, which are *equally contrary* to the laws and safety of all nations.' Jay's Treaty (1794) between Britain and the United States contained a provision for extradition only when offences were similar. Upper Canada's Fugitive Offenders' Act (1833) authorized extradition only when 'such evidence of criminality as, according to the laws of this province, would in the opinion of the Governor ... warrant the apprehension and commitment for trial of such fugitive.' The mere fact that slavery no longer existed in Canada did not make any less criminal a slave's act of arson, murder, or other felony done in furtherance of his escape. These acts, by themselves, would also have been criminal acts in Canada. The mere fact that an extraditable offence had been committed in escaping slavery did not make that act any the less extraditable. There was nothing novel in the comments of the law officers in the Jesse Happy case, and nothing that offered any hope to fugitive slaves.

This was especially apparent in the 1841 application by Arkansas for the return of Nelson Hackett. Before setting out for Canada, Hackett had taken his master's horse and a beaver coat; and from the neighbours he had appropriated a saddle and an expensive watch. The governor of Canada, Sir Charles Bagot, thought that Hackett had taken items superfluous to his needs for escape. Moreover, Bagot was reluctant to turn Canada into 'an asylum for the worst characters provided only that they had been slaves before arriving here.'[17] Nelson Hackett was returned to Arkansas, and to no one's surprise he was promptly re-enslaved. His case had shown just how precarious a refuge Canada could be.

The extradition question came under review during the 1842 treaty negotiations between Britain and the United States. Lord Ashburton, the

British delegate, was aware of the concerns of the anti-slavery lobby, though the possibility of extraditing fugitives from Canada was never specifically discussed. During the course of the negotiations, however, the parties did discuss the *Creole* mutiny. In November 1841 a group of slaves had seized the American ship *Creole* off the Florida coast, killed a man, and forced the ship to sail to the British Bahamas. The American secretary of state, Daniel Webster, argued that the comity of nations required Britain to abstain from interfering with American ships. Lord Ashburton replied that 'certain great principles too deeply rooted in the consciences and sympathies of the people' prevented extradition in these circumstances.[18] Many abolitionists saw universal principles of justice at work in the British refusal to extradite the *Creole* mutineers. The 'higher law' of freedom had justified the slaves' performing any act to escape bondage, and that higher law overrode international treaties.[19]

The British abhorrence of the use of criminal extradition to return escaped slaves was apparent early in the negotiations. In 1840 Lord Palmerston, the foreign secretary, had said that if robbery and horse-theft (the only two crimes he considered a fleeing slave likely to commit) were excluded from the treaty, the fugitives would be safe.[20] Larger issues intervened, however. Both countries wished to resolve boundary disputes in the northeast and to establish law and order along the Canadian frontier. In the end they made no attempt to address the question of the fugitive slaves. Ashburton reported to the foreign secretary that President Tyler was 'very sore and testy about the Creole.' Yet nothing in the treaty guaranteed the Americans that the British would return fugitive slaves. Likewise, the treaty did nothing to exempt escaped slaves from its provisions. In August 1842, when the Webster-Ashburton treaty was signed, robbery was included as an extraditable offence. Stabilizing relations with the Americans apparently outweighed the fears of the anti-slavery lobby. Article x of the treaty provided that in cases of murder, piracy, arson, or forgery a warrant 'may issue' for the fugitive's surrender. The permissive 'may' meant that the surrender of a criminal remained ultimately a political decision. The hidden bombshell in Article x lay in its omitting any definition of terms such as 'murder' or 'robbery.' As Lord Aberdeen, the foreign secretary who supervised the final negotiations of the treaty, astutely observed. 'The treaty of extradition of criminals may lead to some difficulties in defining the character of those Acts which are committed by a Slave in order to obtain his freedom.' His lordship left the resolution of these difficulties to others.[21]

Article x would infuriate slaveholders as well as abolitionists. Senator

Thomas Hart Benton of Missouri feared that the peculiar sentiments of the Canadians would make the extradition of a slave impossible: 'Killing his master in defence of his liberty, is no offence in the eye of British law or people,' he warned. 'No slave will ever be given up for it.'[22] For their part the abolitionists feared that criminal extradition would become a subterfuge to re-enslave freed men. A British abolitionist was horrified to think that Article x could become a 'pledge ... that we will be slavecatchers.' Thomas Clarkson, on behalf of the British and Foreign Anti-Slavery Society, urged that fugitive slaves be completely exempted from the treaty's provisions. Soothing words from the British government allayed the abolitionists' fears, and they were led to believe that the Crown would never give up a slave to a mere warrant of extradition. In Parliament Lord Aberdeen assured the opposition that 'some people had supposed that a fugitive slave might be given up under this treaty. This, he must say, was a most unfounded notion. Not only was a fugitive slave guilty of no crime in endeavouring to escape from a state of bondage but he was entitled to the sympathy and encouragement of all those who were animated by Christian feelings.'[23]

In the years following the ratification of the Webster-Ashburton treaty these assurances seemed to stand up. No fugitive was ever returned to a slave state, but no case came squarely within the terms of the treaty. However, Article x was not as effective a safeguard as the Foreign Office had assured the anti-slavery lobby. A case similar to Anderson's had arisen in 1843. Seven Florida slaves were accused of having killed a white man in Key Biscayne before escaping to the Bahamas. The American extradition request was refused owing to insufficient evidence; however, the Bahamian judges concluded that if 'any such evidence [had] been offered to us, we should of course have considered ourselves bound to receive it, and to issue our warrant for apprehending the offenders.'[24] Clearly, the judges contemplated the extradition of fugitive slaves for a murder committed in the course of escape. In the ensuing diplomatic correspondence, the Americans pressed the view that the 'true intent' of the treaty was 'that the criminality of the act charged should be judged by the laws of the country within whose jurisdiction the act was perpetrated.'[25] Britain never formally accepted this interpretation, and the liability of escaped slaves to answer for acts committed in slavery remained an open question. However, successive American administrations had made it clear that they considered the slaves to be covered by the treaty. Even Lord Ashburton, who considered that acts 'connected with the fact of emancipation' would not be extraditable, conceded to Thomas

Clarkson that 'it is perfectly true that in the surrender of real criminals no distinction can or will be made with respect to colour & condition & therefore the Slave committing crime will be treated like any other person.'[26]

Yet the slave states did not appear eager to test the machinery of extradition. Perhaps only in a case as serious as murder would southern authorities proceed with vigour. As the New Orleans attorney had observed to Laura Haviland in the case of John Anderson, 'the South is determined to have that man.'

In the years after 1854 John Anderson lived quietly in Canada West. He was not prone to violence, but was a circumspect, hard-working young man. Travelling about the province, he eventually learned the trade of mason and plasterer. In about 1858 he bought a house in the small town of Caledonia, Brant County, and seemed ready to fade into obscurity. Respected by his neighbours, Anderson was described as 'rather stout and respectable looking.' His local newspaper, the *Grand River Sachem*, expressed incredulity when his arrest was revealed: 'He is just about the last person we should have accused of murder.'[27]

Any fugitive with a past was wise to keep that past well concealed. Unfortunately, Anderson had become friends with another fugitive named Wynne, who, in a fit of pique over some quarrel with Anderson, had informed the magistrate of Onandaga Township that Anderson was a wanted man. According to Wynne, he and Anderson had been friends in Windsor in 1854, and Anderson had bragged of the stabbing incident. In March 1860 the Onandaga magistrate prepared a criminal information concerning Anderson's stabbing of an unknown Missourian and presented it to a justice of the peace, William Mathews.[28] Wynne also mentioned that Officer Port of Windsor knew of all the circumstances, and had been searching for Anderson for years.

Anderson was tapping maple-syrup trees when he was taken into custody by one of Mathews's sheriffs. Samuel Port was sent for, and he identified Anderson as the killer. How Port could identify Anderson in view of his inability to capture him in 1854 was inexplicable. Indeed, it is questionable whether he ever laid eyes on Anderson before 1860. In any event, Port's identification was acceptable to Mathews. Port had had the foresight to retain the warrant for Anderson's arrest that had been sworn in 1854. He was undoubtedly aware that Missouri's thousand-dollar reward was still outstanding; sensing that if he moved fast he could earn a great deal of money, he notified a Detroit detective, James A. Gunning, of

Anderson's arrest. In later months Mathews's enemies, and especially the *Toronto Globe*, would pillory him for acting 'the part of the kidnapper for the Missouri slave-catchers.'[29] In reality it was Wynne who had laid the charge, and Samuel Port who notified the American authorities of the fugitive's whereabouts. In view of the accusations against Anderson, William Mathews would have been delinquent in his duty if he had not had him arrested.

Soon after the arrest, Magistrate Mathews interrogated his prisoner. Anderson made no attempt to deny the accusaton or to be evasive, but simply told Mathews that while he was escaping 'he was pursued by several men, one of whom (whose name he does not know) came up with him and attempted to take him: that being afraid if taken, he would be severely punished, he stabbed the man with a pocket knife ... He never heard till his arrest that the party had died.'[30]

If the extradition of Anderson was to succeed, it was essential that the authorities in Howard Country be informed and the necessary charges obtained. James Gunning knew that a handsome bounty was waiting for him in the Brantford jail, and he sent a letter to the Digges family to explain the situation. Getting the essential information from Howard county was no easy task. Even though Detective Gunning had engineered other extraditions, and was to be the mastermind of these proceedings, it took several letters and an exchange of telegrams before the message that Seneca Digges's killer was in jail in Canada was received in Missouri. The family's first act was to get in touch with Washington and ask that extradition proceedings be initiated. The Digges family sent an agent to represent them in Brantford. The agent arrived in Detroit on a Saturday evening and telegraphed the Brantford jail to inform Mathews that he would be there the following Monday. But he was too late; Anderson had been released two hours before the telegram arrived.[31]

Mathews had already held Anderson for four weeks on a remand, and he was becoming uneasy about detaining him any longer. He sought the advice of Justice Archibald McLean, who was in Brantford for the spring assizes. McLean indicated that the prisoner should be freed. Alerted to the case by newspaper reports, Canadian abolitionists also began to pressure the Brantford magistrate. Anderson's plight had already been reported in provincial newspapers, and the *Globe* expressed the pious hope that 'every care will be taken that he is not delivered to the United States authorities for such a crime.'[32] Without even knowing the circumstances of the killing, abolitionists were eagerly lining up in support of the fugitive.

John Scoble, for one, had rushed to Brantford as soon as he heard of the case. Scoble, a passionate abolitionist, had been the secretary of the British and Foreign Anti-Slavery Society. In 1843 he had led the fight against Article x of the Webster-Ashburton treaty. On behalf of the British and Foreign Anti-Slavery Society, Scoble had drafted a petition demanding that no fugitive slave surrendered to the United States be reduced to slavery.[33] During his term as secretary his egocentric style had caused splits in the anti-slavery movement in both Britain and Canada, and had led one detractor to call him 'a self-willed, tyrannically-minded, narrow-souled, clever bigot.'[34] In 1852, when Scoble came to Canada, he became the superintendent of the Dawn settlement for escaped slaves. Not only did he mismanage the affairs of the settlement, he proved to be a white liberal of the most paternalistic sort who was not able to work with blacks as equals. To his credit, Scoble was wholly devoted to the anti-slavery struggle and would be a key figure in securing Anderson's ultimate release. After talking with Anderson, Scoble urged him and his lawyer to seek a writ of habeas corpus. (Anderson's lawyer was unwilling to ask for the writ, but it is interesting to note that it was Scoble who first proposed this action.) In any event, Anderson's release at the end of April obviated the need for habeas corpus.

Upon his arrival in Brantford on 30 April 1860, James Gunning swore an information that John Anderson did wilfully murder Seneca Digges. To no avail: Anderson, once again a fugitive, was nowhere to be found. James Gunning was not about to abandon a thousand-dollar reward easily, and together with another Detroit detective, Julius Blodgett, and a local Indian tracker he began to scour Canada West. By the end of August Blodgett succeeded in finding their quarry living in a community of blacks in the small town of Simcoe in Norfolk County. On 1 September Blodgett instructed a Brantford police officer, Richard Yeoward, to arrest Anderson and secure him in the Simcoe jail. As an added bonus to his Simcoe trip, Officer Blodgett recognized another black in the town as a murderer wanted in Ohio, and had him arrested as well.[35] Neither Anderson nor his Simcoe friends were about to accept recapture peacefully. The arresting officer, Yeoward, charged Anderson with resisting arrest and stabbing him in the breast during a scuffle. This stabbing incident must not have been very serious, for no charges were ever proceeded with.

While Mathews attempted to regain his prisoner, Anderson's friends surrounded the Simcoe jail. There were dark hints that they would release him by force. The *Norfolk Messenger* reported that emotions ran high: 'The colored people in town have apparently thought that there was no chance for justice anywhere else,'[36] and resisted returning their comrade to Mathews's custody. Mathews was determined to have the charge dealt with in Brantford, however, and he sent the Brant County attorney to Simcoe to secure Anderson's return. Mathews ordered a posse of police to accompany the attorney, 'which precaution was deemed necessary as there was good reason to fear a rescue.'[37] On 27 September the Simcoe magistrates overrode the protests of Anderson's counsel and decided to return the fugitive to the Brant County authorities. On the night before Anderson was to be transferred to Brantford, the anxious blacks who had been camped out around the jail attempted to free him. Apparently, they had been incited by a white abolitionist, Samuel Tisdale, to make the attempt. The 'rapidity of the constables' movements' dissuaded them, and the rescue was abandoned.

The following morning the Brant County police took charge of Anderson. Following closely in the wake of the posse were Anderson's Simcoe friends. They were there to ensure that there were no unauthorized detours to the American border. On several occasions (the kidnapping of a young black man, Louis Snow, being the most famous) fugitive slaves had been returned to American authorities without benefit of legal proceedings. American law officers were finding it expeditious to hire Canadian police to abduct wanted men. To discourage these abductions, the Hamilton Chief of Police was convicted of kidnapping Snow and fined fifty pounds.[38] The caution displayed by Anderson's friends in seeing that he was not kidnapped was warranted. After arriving in Brantford, the Simcoe blacks decided to stay in town to make sure that their compatriot was not hastily deported.

It now remained for Mathews to conduct a formal investigation of the charges against Anderson and to determine whether he should be committed for extradition. In the meantime he ordered that Anderson be kept handcuffed and under constant guard. Although Anderson was permitted to see his lawyer, none of his black friends or even his minister, the Reverend Mr Hawkins, were permitted to visit him. According to one report Hawkins was rudely pushed out of the Brantford jail and told that 'the Sherriff had given strict orders that no nigger should be permitted to see him.'[39] In William Mathews's mind there existed little doubt of his prisoner's guilt. Mathews alleged (without proof) that Anderson had been involved in a knifing incident a few years earlier, that 'he had stabbed a negro in a drunken brawl,' that he had written to his fellow blacks in Missouri, urging them to rise up 'to murder their masters right and left, and come off to Canada, where they would be quite safe.'

Finally, he had 'applied his knife with murderous intent to Mr Yeoward.' Mathews had sized up his man. The abolitionists were trying to free a violent criminal *'from the hands of justice, thereby, cheating the gallows* of its prey and setting him free to extend his Bowie-knife practice to Canadians instead of Southern slaveholders. A sweet creature this is, truly, to make so much ado about!'[40]

As for the prisoner, Mathews's 'scoundrel' lay handcuffed and alone in jail, wondering why he was being arrested, released, and rearrested. He could only shake his head at this strange, rule-bound society. He later said that 'he never knew there was *so much law* in the world as he has found in Canada.'[41]

4

A Cause Célèbre

The Anderson case was about to be heard in a town in which the races – white, native, and black – lived in uneasy coexistence. The blacks who surrounded the Brantford jail symbolized hostilities that occasionally flared up in the community. Mostly white, mostly Protestant, the mechanics and tradesmen of Brantford were building themselves a prosperous little town. Where a generation before there had been wilderness, Messrs Ganson and Waterous were now producing the latest style of steam-engines. The growing town also attracted new workers to its mills and factories, and this did not make for a genteel society: 'The timid seldom relished the prospect of spending even so much as a night in Brantford, so uproarious did the denizens of bars and lodgings become in the course of the night's carousal. Itinerant fistfights between Irishmen and Covenanters and brawls between Indians and Americans ... understandably frightened off many of the timorous.'[1]

The most recent presence in the county, and a presence that was frequently resented, was that of the fugitive slaves. An elderly white mail-carrier was murdered by three blacks in 1859, and the subsequent hanging of two of the killers was the first to take place in Brantford. The killing had sparked calls in the groggeries to stop having 'niggers about among white folks ... Canada would be much better without them.'[2] Racial innuendoes even became a feature of a mayoral contest when it was alleged that one candidate had 'expressed a wish that all colored people in Brantford might be driven out of the country and sold into slavery.'[3] Perhaps it was fortunate for Anderson that the extradition hearing would require no jury, and that Magistrate Mathews's decision would have to be approved by the government.

To some people William Mathews seemed an odd choice to determine a fellow human being's fate. In 1837 he had been a mere bootmaker and the 'acknowledged leader of the malcontents of the village of Brantford.'[4] During the 1837 uprising Mathews had led a tiny band in a foolhardy attempt to seize Brantford. After the collapse of the rebellion he had gone into a short exile in the United States. When the rebels regained respectability, Mathews again took part in political life and eventually became the mayor of Brantford. His political style can charitably be described as forceful. During the 1857 mayoral campaign the Reformers alleged that Mathews had 'not only obstructed the poll, but assaulted the electors.'[5] By 1860 the one-time rebel had been appointed a justice of the peace. Mathews owed his ascendancy to his membership in the Conservative party and the patronage of the party leader, Attorney General John A. Macdonald. The opposition Reformers were a powerful block in Brant County, and their newspaper, the *Expositor*, frequently pilloried Mathews. In 1859 he was alleged to have beaten a defenceless prisoner. 'Oh brace, brave Mathews,' mocked the *Expositor*. 'And this is the man who pollutes the bench with his presence.'[6] Even as a magistrate William Mathews remained a controversial political figure.

The justice of the peace wasted no time in dealing with his prisoner. Hours after Anderson arrived back in Brantford he was charged with the murder of Seneca Digges. The county attorney, G.R. Van Norman, and a Mr McKerlie appeared on behalf of the Crown. The prisoner faced a stolid row of Missourians who were prepared to present evidence against him. The state of Missouri had indeed posted a one-thousand-dollar reward for Anderson's return, and agreed to pay the expenses of the witnesses. One family member, F.W. Digges, was now mayor of Glasgow, Missouri, and he undoubtedly had kept the state officials aware of the case.

Extradition hearings were still rare, but it happened that in the previous month Mathews had presided over the extradition of another American fugitive. On that occasion he had asked the attorney general how he should handle the case. Macdonald had replied that he could accept written depositions or oral testimony, but in any event 'you should require evidence of criminality sufficient to sustain a charge according to the laws of this Province' before extradition should follow.[7] It was this guideline, so simple in appearance, that was to prove so difficult to apply in practice.

The hearing began with the testimony of a Missouri carpenter, William C. Baker, who had known Anderson in Missouri and was able to identify him out of a group of three black men. Baker was a friend of Digges, and had visited his deathbed and heard him recount the story of the pursuit and stabbing. Remarkably, Baker's testimony omitted any reference to a second stab wound. He had observed only 'one cut in his right side.'[8] This was a startling omission which the defence failed to exploit. Under further questioning from Van Norman he also insisted that Digges was conscious and not in a delirium at the time he described the incident.

Although it was still early in the day, Anderson's defence counsel, G.M. Wilson, asked that the case be adjourned. Anderson's principal counsel, Samuel B. Freeman, was expected in the morning, and he would handle the case from that point on. Mathews agreed. About an hour after the adjournment Freeman and the Simcoe abolitionist, Tisdale, appeared and asked that the hearing proceed. Reluctantly, Mathews consented. Also at Freeman's request, Baker was recalled to the witness stand. So far, Baker had only identified Anderson and related some of Digges's dying comments. Further examination produced information that impugned the prisoner's character. In answer to Van Norman, Baker observed that Anderson was 'savage and ill-disposed.' Freeman followed up this line of questioning, and Baker added that 'his public reputation was bad for stealing and being a thief.'[9] Yet Baker could offer no instances of Anderson's violent conduct, and in the only confrontation he described no blows had been struck. Nevertheless, the allegation had been made that Anderson was a violent character.

The next witness was the deceased's eldest son, Thomas. He could not identify Anderson, and he had not been present at the stabbing. All he could recount to the magistrate was his father's dying recollection of the 'cutting affair.' On that day his father had stopped a black man, who told him that he was trying to get another planter to buy him. 'It looked suspicious living so far off; he must be a runaway.' Digges felt obliged to stop the slave, for 'he could not allow him to go without a pass, as he would be held responsible.'[10] In a slave society a planter such as Digges was under a positive duty to apprehend runaways. When the slave broke and ran, Digges, his slaves, and his son Ben pursued him. After some time the black man suddenly appeared, ran at the planter, and stabbed him in the chest. As Digges turned, he tripped and fell and was again stabbed, this time in the back. Thomas observed that his father was a 'delicate man, slim and small,' and was armed only with a paw-paw stick. Everyone in the courtroom could see that John Anderson was a strong, robust young man. Freeman chose not to cross-examine Thomas Digges, and the case closed for the day.

The following day, the hearing began with the testimony of the Brant County constable, B. Hazelhurst. He told the magistrate that Anderson had admitted to cutting a man in his escape from slavery. Hazelhurst's testimony added little to the case against the prisoner. The same was not true of the next piece of evidence. Van Norman sought to admit a deposition sworn by Seneca Digges's slave Phil. The case against Anderson had come down to this one crucial piece of evidence, which both identified the killer and placed him at the scene of the murder; and that evidence depended on the testimony of a slave. Phil was the only person who could identify John Anderson and who could swear that he had wielded the knife that had killed Seneca Digges. Obviously, the Missourians would have difficulty getting the witness to testify. If Phil was brought to Brantford, he would become free the moment he stepped on Canadian soil, and probably would lose his enthusiasm for testifying against a fellow freeman. Therefore Phil had been taken to a Missouri lawyer, J.A. Holliday, before whom a sworn deposition was completed. From a tactical perspective, Freeman should have objected strenuously to the introduction of this depositiion. It meant, for one thing, that he would be stopped from cross-examining Phil. How could he determine whether Phil had been coerced or paid to make the deposition? If the deposition was admitted, Freeman would lose his opportunity to cast doubt on Phil's recollections. Moreover, according to Missouri law, a black's testimony was tainted and could be used only in a case involving a fellow black. If black testimony was so suspect in Missouri, why should it be persuasive in Canada?

Amazingly enough, Freeman made no objections to the deposition. Phil's evidence was admitted, and it showed conclusively that Anderson was the fugitive who stabbed Seneca Digges. Phil had been acquainted with Anderson and his wife Maria in Howard County. When Anderson had tried to escape from Digges and his slaves, Phil had joined the pursuit. He recalled Seneca Digges's calling out that whoever caught the runaway could keep the reward. After recounting the lengthy pursuit, Phil described the knifing: 'At last master met the negro, and I saw him cut master twice with a knife.' When Digges's slaves persisted in the pursuit, Anderson turned on them and 'said he would kill us if we came near him.'[11] How close was Phil to the incident that he could report it in such detail? Why, if he had seen his master struck down and stabbed twice, had he not gone to render assistance? A thorough cross-examination might have cast considerable doubt on Phil's firsthand view of events. When Freeman was later roasted by the press for this tactical error, he responsed that he had to admit Phil's deposition because it showed 'the determination and ferocity with which Digges was acting.'[12] It showed nothing of the kind; in fact, because Freeman had cast away any chance to rebut or contradict Phil, the slave's evidence stood as a glaring condemnation of his client.

Next to testify was J.A. Holliday, the Howard County lawyer. Unable to identify Anderson or discuss the killing, he could only inform the magistrate of the provisions of Missouri law. According to the slave act, any white man could apprehend a runaway who was more than twenty miles from his master. Freeman chose not to cross-examine. At the time, Holliday's evidence may have seemed of little consequence. However, he had established a vital point that the Crown would later exploit: Seneca Digges possessed a clear legal authority to apprehend a runaway.

Last to testify was Benjamin Digges. Now fifteen, Ben recounted the knifing incident in much the same form as his elder brother. He had to admit that 'the prisoner is about the colour and size of the man, but I would not swear he is the man.' Freeman cross-examined to no great effect, and the case closed. Mathews had heard enough. To his mind, the facts indicated that a murder had occurred. Mathews and two other magistrates, Henry Yardington and James Langtry, signed the warrant of commitment. It only remained for the governor general to sign the order returning John Anderson to the Missouri authorities.

Three days after the commitment Anderson introduced his own petition.[13] It was true that he was a runaway, for he had 'always felt that he had a right to his freedom.' Unwilling to hide anything, he readily admitted that the testimony of the Missourians was true, that 'at the moment he was looking for success, Mister Digges appeared before him.' There was no choice; Seneca Digges stood between him and freedom. Anderson begged the governor general not to send him back to Missouri, for he had 'only used such force as was necessary.' The government received this petition, but was already looking for a way to transfer this embarrassing question to the courts.

Canada West had taken little notice of the Brantford proceedings. The *Brantford Expositor* observed, 'The investigation was held, and conducted fairly, fully and legally by the magistrate.' Striking a rare note of approbation, the paper declared that 'when [Mathews] discharges his public duties faithfully, honestly, and fearlessly, as he has done in this extradition case, we are willing to accord to him the well-earned mead of praise.'[14]

Anderson's tribulations were not widely reported. In September 1860 the province was in the grip of a royal mania as Albert Edward, the Prince of Wales, made the first official visit of a member of the royal family to Britain's North American possessions. The public avidly read details of the prince's progress, and royalty-starved Canadians went to great lengths to get a glimpse of their future king. Yet the prince's visit also revealed the deep animosities that split Canadian society. It was rumoured that the prince had paid homage to the French Catholics of Canada East, and orangemen hotly insisted on similar courtesies for their order. The Duke of Newcastle, the leader of the prince's entourage and the colonial secretary, refused to permit his charge to be part of any demonstrations. In Toronto the Prince could not even attend church without Orangemen erecting their arches outside the cathedral and forcing the royal carriage to career wildly through the streets searching for an avenue that had no arch above it.

The prince's tumultuous visit was only a symptom of a badly divided society. Canada East (Quebec) was fiercely French-speaking and Catholic; Canada West (Ontario) was equally fiercely English-speaking and Protestant. Ever since the Canadian provinces had been united in 1841, politicians had had to accommodate not only Reformers and Conservatives but English and French, Protestants and Catholics. Accommodation was always difficult, and during the 1850s a series of coalitions tried to provide a stable government. In September 1854 a combination of opposition groups, including tories and dissident reformers, created a 'Liberal-Conservative' party and formed a government under Sir Allan MacNab.

In 1856 John A. Macdonald replaced MacNab as the leader of the Canada West branch of the Liberal-Conservatives. Macdonald, an energetic Kingston lawyer, resolved a lingering dispute over the secularization of the clergy reserves and reformed the provincial laws on usury and imprisonment for debt. A consummate politician, able to choose the appropriate moment to foil an enemy or make a valuable friend, Macdonald came to dominate Canada West's administration. His success in public life was all the more remarkable in view of his tragic personal circumstances. His first wife had become an invalid soon after their marriage and had died in 1858. Perhaps to forget his family troubles, Macdonald became a hard drinker. Nevertheless, he was the most capable leader in the province, and after forming a coalition with the 'bleus' of Canada East, Macdonald and the French-Canadian leader George-Étienne Cartier were able to form a workable majority in the legislature. Yet sectional rivalries continually threatened to topple Macdonald and Cartier's fragile administration. Their principal opponent was the editor of the *Toronto Globe*, George Brown.

After the disintegration of the old Reform party in the early 1850s, Brown had re-created a liberal Reform party in Canada West. This party was founded on its opposition to Macdonald's 'sellout' to the French Catholics, and particularly to the creation of separate Catholic schools in Protestant-dominated Canada West. Jingoistic appeals on behalf of a threatened Protestantism made the Reformers a force in Canada West. George Brown accused the Cartier-Macdonald administration of 'sacrificing the higher interests of the country at the shrine of Roman priestcraft,' and warned that through Macdonald 'Rome openly threatens inroads upon their liberties.'[15] One Catholic Reformer, Thomas D'Arcy McGee, begged Brown to stop pandering to religious hatreds: 'Why cannot the *Globe* state its own strong case, without using offensive epithets such as "Priestcraft," "Popish," "Romish," "Jesuits" [?]'[16] Brown's *Globe* was also a powerful voice in the propaganda war against slavery, and especially in the defence of John Anderson. *Globe* editorials condemned the Fugitive Slave Act, southern slavery, and Canadian racists in equal measure. Thomas Henning, the first secretary of the Anti-Slavery Society of Canada, who wrote editorials for the *Globe* until 1854, was married to Brown's sister Isabella. Apparently, Brown found it convenient to champion the oppressed slaves of the distant South but somewhat more difficult to tolerate the all-too-near Catholics of Canada.

Yet Brown's program was not without its positive aspects. He also advocated the annexation to Canada of the Northwest Territories and fair representation for Canada West's voters. In 1859 he called for a convention of the Reform party to discuss the possibility of a dual federation of the Canadas. By the force of his personality Brown persuaded that convention to accept a resolution that called for the dissolution of the existing union and the federation of the two provinces.[17] Although Brown was a champion to the Reformers of Canada West, his support in the French Catholic east was understandably small. By following moderate policies and deferring decisions the Cartier-Macdonald ministry kept the unwieldy polity of Canada together. None the less, dissatisfaction was so widespread that a collapse of the union always remained a possibility.

After the Price of Wales left British America to continue his journey in the

United States, the Anderson case was suddenly wrenched from obscurity. Attorney General Macdonald was now faced with deciding whether to return Anderson to Missouri, and thus a short and unpleasant fate, or to defy the Americans. To return Anderson would give Brown and the Reformers a chance to show Macdonald as a tool of the diabolical slaveholders. To refuse to extradite Anderson might constitute a repudiation of the Webster-Ashburton treaty. A provincial election was due in 1861, and it seemed likely that the issue would destroy the already precarious Cartier-Macdonald administration.

In the days following the Brantford hearing, Macdonald corresponded with Freeman. They considered various alternatives. Freeman suggested that the attorney general look at the law and see if it was possible to discharge Anderson forthwith. Freeman felt that 'a man who takes the life of another to prevent his being carried back to slavery' could not legally be guilty of murder. At the most his crime might be manslaughter, which was not an extraditable offence. Macdonald replied that he could not simply release the prisoner: 'I have come to the conclusion with great regret, but without any doubt existing in my mind that this party has committed the crime of murder; under these circumstances all I can do is to give you every assistance in testing the question before the Courts or a Judge by Habeas Corpus.'[18] Freeman had previously warned Macdonald that 'counsel for the informants [appear] to be confident that their clients will get the *Niggar*.' Because the case was a novel one, the matter should go before the judges on a writ of habeas corpus.[19] Macdonald and Freeman agreed to bring the case before Queen's Bench at the end of the judicial term. One matter of utmost importance remained. The prisoner was a simple plasterer and quite unable to afford his counsel fees. The attorney general assured Freeman that the government would cover the payment of all legal costs. A canny politician, Macdonald was eager to spend taxpayers' money in the defence of Anderson so that he could honestly maintain that he was in full co-operation with Anderson's defence. By placing himself on both sides of the issue Macdonald could be seen as prosecuting the law, but in so liberal a manner that the fugitive was given every legal recourse.

Macdonald's adroit handling of the issue could never deflect all criticism. George Brown's *Globe* would eventually seize upon the case and show the 'corruptionist' administration for what it was. Besides, 1860 had not been a kind year for George Brown and his Reformers. Brown had tried to arouse public indignation at the government's intention to spend public funds to assist in the building of the Grand Trunk Railway.

According to the *Globe*, Macdonald and his minions were profiting from these grants and thereby 'mining their way ... into the public treasury.'[20] But the Grand Trunk would provide year-round connections for many centres in the province, and was generally perceived as a work of necessity. Moreover, the legislative session of 1860 had shown the Reform party to be badly divided. The caucus expressed dissatisfaction with the 1859 convention, and many Reformers favoured an out-and-out dissolution of the union. At this prospect Brown threatened to resign, and he kept the party together only with great difficulty. Macdonald rejoiced at the Reformers' disarray, and smugly pointed out to the legislature that there was no real Reform party, only 'a number of atoms accidentally placed together but without any principle of adhesion and indeed without any principle at all.'[21] By 1860 the Reformers were petulant and divided, and their leader was exhausted. The Anderson case was an opportunity for the Reformers to present a simple issue to the people, a chance to unite again under a cause, and above all, an opportunity to attack Macdonald.

The storm of public controversy over the Anderson case was initiated by the *Hamilton Times*. The editor, George Sheppard, was a Clear Grit radical, a believer in American-style elective democracy. His radicalism had caused him to break with Brown and the mainstream Reformers, and he became the editor of the Hamilton paper to advance his own views. The *Times* played upon widespread abolitionist sentiments in Canada to generate sympathy for Anderson and scorn for his prosecutors. Immediately after the Brantford hearing in September, the Hamilton *Times* excoriated both Mathews and Van Norman and demanded Anderson's immediate release.[22] According to the *Times*, there was no doubt who the villains of the piece were: 'By order of the ruffian Mathews (Mr. John A. Macdonald's Brantford entertainer), the poor fellow was at his arrest loaded with irons, and he has now suffered a rigorous incarceration of nearly two months; during which time he has been subjected to such severe discipline that his health is rapidly breaking up.'[23]

It was not until 14 November, only days before the habeas corpus hearing, that the *Globe* took notice of the Anderson case. While the editorialist taunted the Americans, most of his venom was reserved for the attorney general. The fugitive's fate should have 'elicited sympathy even from callous Ministerialists.' Instead, Macdonald was responsible for holding an innocent man in jail. 'Two months' imprisonment in gaol, heavily ironed, may seem trifling to some people,' said the *Globe*, 'especially where a "nigger" is concerned.'

Two weeks later the *Globe* articulated the case against the attorney general. The Webster-Ashburton treaty made no provision for the transfer of extradition questions to judges by way of application for habeas corpus. The decision was a political one, and Macdonald had no right to 'shift the responsibility of a decision from their own shoulders where the Treaty has placed it, to those of the Judges, where the Treaty, for good and sufficient reasons, has not placed it.' All but forgotten was the fact that it had been the abolitionist John Scoble who had first urged the application for habeas corpus. Not only was Macdonald condemned for shirking 'the duty which the law has imposed,' he was also suspected of acting in concert with the vile southern slaveholders: 'But, says the Attorney General, we must recognize the slave code; we must admit that it has some force even in Canada – so much force that it compels us to deliver up for execution as a murderer a man whom we believe and who would be held by our law, to have committed justifiable homicide!'[24] The government was portrayed as helping slaveowners recover an escaped bondsman for a horrible execution and as a warning to others. The Anderson extradition case was a raw, emotional issue which the *Globe* used to blacken Macdonald as thoroughly as it could. The fire-storm of controversy ignited by the *Hamilton Times* was vigorously fanned by the *Globe*, and the legal complexities of the case were conveniently ignored.

Liberal editors across the province used the case to highlight the moral superiority of British Americans. Many asked why it was necessary to surrender Anderson when recently the Americans had refused to surrender criminals to Canadian justice. In January 1859 a U.S. marshal had shot a fugitive in Port Sarnia and dragged the fatally wounded man to Michigan. Canadians were outraged. The Americans replied that the marshal was only doing his duty and was not liable to be extradited.[25] The *Kingston British Whig* observed that American authorities never returned deserted British soliders for punishment no matter what their crime. Why should Canada surrender Anderson?[26]

Yet even the Anti-Slavery Society of Canada might have been unsure of the weight of Anderson's case. In the wake of John Brown's disastrous raid on Harpers Ferry, Virginia, in 1858, the American government had inquired after Canadian residents who were implicated in the raid. George Brown had consulted the society's lawyer, Oliver Mowat, who replied that these persons might well be subject to extradition. During the Rebellion of 1837 the British government had treated as pirates the Americans who had invaded Canada during peacetime. The Canadian government demanded that those who had not been captured be returned for court-martial. The same laws applied to Brown's raiders, and Mowat was afraid that in a strict legal sense they were liable to be handed over.[27] They could avoid extradition only by trying to characterize their acts as 'political offences.' The American authorities did not press the request, however. The significance of Mowat's opinion lay in the concession by one of Canada's leading abolitionists that acts committed in resisting slavery could lead to extradition. This was a position that the liberal press and especially the *Globe* would never publicly concede.

The *Globe* had made a telling point in criticizing Macdonald for relying upon the habeas corpus hearing. After the magistrates issued Anderson's warrant of commitment, it was for Macdonald, not the judges, to decide whether he should be extradited. Nevertheless, the writ of habeas corpus was available to a prisoner in Anderson's situation. The writ was an order issued by a court calling on the sheriff to bring a prisoner before the court. Once a prisoner was in front of the judges, they would then determine whether he was being held according to the law or whether he should be released. Habeas corpus was a remedy that enabled any prisoner to have the legality of his detention reviewed. The writ had traditionally existed in English law, but after it was given statutory recognition by the Habeas Corpus Act (1679) it became one of the fundamental bulwarks of a free society. Even with the right of habeas corpus the extradition of Anderson was primarily a governmental decision, but in view of the public indignation over the case Macdonald was eager to send the issue to the courts.

By now the Anderson case had become an international concern. On 2 October 1860 the United States State Department formally asked the British ambassador in Washington, Lord Lyons, for Anderson's extradition. The British embassy forwarded this request to London, and the governor general of Canada, Sir Edmund Head, was instructed to return Anderson, this 'man of colour,' to Missouri.[28] So far the case was strictly routine. The first unusual note was struck when the American secretary of state, Lewis Cass, advised Lord Lyons that Senator James S. Green of Missouri was most interested in the case and was afraid that the prisoner was about to be discharged.[29] The British embassy hastily contacted Canada and learned that Anderson was being held pending the habeas corpus hearing. For the moment the Americans were content.

Lord Lyons was trying to maintain peaceful relations between Britain and America, and he must have occasionally felt that it was a losing effort. During the Prince of Wales's tour through the United States, Lord Lyons's superior, the Duke of Newcastle took the opportunity to talk with influential Americans. He especially sought out William Seward, a dominant figure in the Republican party and the man Newcastle considered likely to become president in the 1860 election. Festering disputes concerning boundary claims in the northwest and compensation for the Hudson's Bay Company had disrupted relations between the countries. Recently, the Americans had sent troops to the British-held San Juan Islands. William Seward had speculated whether a war with Great Britain over the islands might be just the tonic to cure American domestic ills. Perhaps the imminent secession of the southern states could be delayed, or even avoided, if the country united in a war against Britain.[30] Newcastle was shocked at this byzantine strategy, which seemed to him an indication that peaceful relations between the two countries were in a precarious state. Seward's propensity for making speeches in which 'he looked to the acquisition of British America' increased British concerns about American expansionism.[31] For its part, Britain did not want to be the source of any new friction with the United States. Perhaps that was why Lord Lyons was so quick to accommodate the American request for Anderson's return. But the extradition of an ordinary criminal for punishment and the delivery of an escaped slave to certain death were two quite different matters. The first act was proper, the second unthinkable. This issue would test Britain's desire for peace against what the British public would condemn as a supremely immoral act.

Even before the Brantford hearing the American public suspected that the Canadians would refuse to return Anderson. The *Detroit Daily Advertiser* wondered whether 'the fact that Anderson is a fugitive slave [is] being used by the Canadian authorities as an excuse for requiring the strictest proof that he is a murderer.'[32] Americans were particularly enraged when the black man arrested at Simcoe with Anderson for the Ohio murder was released because of lack of proof. 'So the ends of justice are defeated again,' fumed the Detroit newspapers, 'and that too, by people who complain so often of the obnoxious presence of negroes in their country.'[33]

Southern opinions of Canadian abolitionism were much harsher. It was a source of great resentment in the south that John Brown had planned his slave insurrection from a Canadian haven. Governor Henry Wise of Virginia had even warned that a war on abolitionists would be carried to the black-welcoming Canadian provinces. A southern newspaper, the *Baltimore American*, recognized the Anderson case as a significant one, and stressed the deliberate nature of the Digges killing – the white planter had been stabbed while he was lying defenceless on the ground. It was important to the south that assassins like Anderson be returned to face their justly deserved punishment.[34]

Public attention in three nations was now drawn to the prisoner in the Brantford jail. Abolitionists in Britain, Canada, and the United States were determined that he should not be sent back to Missouri. The British were especially sensitive to maintain the integrity of their territory as a refuge for escaped slaves. To many Americans the Anderson case proved that the British and Canadians were eager to give asylum to fugitives from American justice. The Anderson case had become what the *Globe* would call one of the 'cause célèbres of the present era.'[35] Even the *New York Times* would refer to 'The Canadian Fugitive Slave Case – now become a cause célèbre.'[36] The *Sarnia Observer* reported that 'the Anderson Extradition Case is causing greater excitement than anything that has occurred in Canada since the burning of the Parliament House.'[37] It was in this emotional climate that Magistrate Mathews sent his charge to Toronto to stand before the judges on the writ of habeas corpus.

5

Argument and Pleading

In Toronto's venerable Osgoode Hall, three of Canada's finest lawyers were arrayed to argue the Anderson case. At age forty-six Samuel Black Freeman, Anderson's defender, was an established practitioner in Hamilton. A devout Reformer, Freeman had been a follower of the party's former leader, Robert Baldwin. Freeman had already served in the legislature, but he would leave his mark in the courts: 'in the art of examining and cross-examining witnesses, and of pleading causes before a jury, he had few equals.'[1] At the Oxford assizes of 1860 Freeman defended a farmer accused of forging a note; a conviction would have meant ruin for his client. Freeman pleaded with the jury 'eloquently and effectively' that the signature was genuine. Both the judge and the jury were convinced and acquitted the accused.[2] In 1859 Freeman had defended the 'Silver Creek murderer' at a sensational trial during the Halton assizes. Freeman gave an eloquent jury address in which he stressed that the evidence against his client was circumstantial and that a murder charge should be established 'with mathematical precision.' He concluded with a folksy exhortation: 'Go home to-night and lay your heads upon your pillow with a conscience unstained with a crime – a conscience free from the sin of sending an innocent man to the gallows.'[3] After only twenty minutes' deliberation the jury acquitted Freeman's client. Despite his ability to sway a jury, Freeman rarely appeared in the reported appeal cases of the period. He was not renowned for his facility at arguing fine points of law. Unfortunately for the defence, this was precisely the talent that would be needed at the Anderson hearing.

Freeman was about to confront two of the most skilled lawyers in the province. Henry Eccles was recognized as the 'leader of the bar in Toronto.'[4] A gentle, courtly barrister, Eccles was highly skilled in presenting arguments and appeared regularly in appeal cases. The jewel in the Crown's case was Robert Harrison. A young man of thirty-three and a practitioner for only five years, Harrison was well on his way to becoming the foremost lawyer in Canada West.[5] Because of his skill in synthesizing and explaining the law, Harrison had become Canada's Blackstone. While still a law clerk he had compiled and published a digest of court decisions. He possessed a unique ability to summarize the law in a manner other lawyers found useful. In 1854 he was appointed chief clerk or deputy to the provincial attorney general, and he continued in this office until 1859. He quickly became indispensable in the conduct of criminal prosecutions. In all cases in which the government was threatened, Harrison represented the Crown. Even after Harrison left the government for more profitable private practice, Macdonald had such respect for his abilities that he was retained specifically to argue the Crown's brief in the Anderson case.

Finally, on 24 November 1860, Anderson was delivered up to the Toronto jailer, G.L. Allen, on a writ of habeas corpus to appear before Chief Justice Robinson and Justices McLean and Burns. The prisoner himself appeared in court wearing a new suit of clothes supplied by his friends. Before the proceedings began he had the chance to thank them for their help. His only complaint was that his friends had been prevented by Mathews from seeing him.[6] None the worse for his imprisonment, Anderson appeared to be a well-built man, about five feet six inches tall with 'broad shoulders and ... an intelligent looking countenance.' Others described him as a 'fine, athletic, intelligent looking man.'[7] Anderson's substantial number of Toronto supporters included not only the local blacks but the many well-to-do whites of the Anti-Slavery Society. Together they could mount an impressive show of public support for the fugitive.

Toronto, the principal city of Canada West, was the judicial and business capital of the western half of the province. By the time of the extradition hearing it had an estimated population of 44,000, and had begun to lose the rough edges of smaller centres like Brantford. Almost 1,000 blacks lived in Toronto, and there was a remarkable absence of overt segregation in the city.[8] During the past ten years Toronto had absorbed a huge influx of Irish Catholics and the troubles between these newcomers and local Protestants overshadowed any animosity towards the black arrivals.[9] As a measure of its sophistication, Toronto even boasted a social organization for lawyers, the 'Osgoode Club,' which debated legal topics for the edification of the students. On the day of the extradition hearing the Osgoode Club posted a notice of the question to be discussed at its next meeting: 'A slave, having escaped from his master in the Southern States, is pursued, and, as the only means of avoiding recapture, slays him … [He] is demanded by the United States' Government under the Ashburton Treaty. Is Canada bound, under the said Treaty, to yield to their demand?'[10] The question may have been an interesting one to prospective lawyers. To Anderson and his friends the issue was far from academic.

Samuel Freeman began his argument by reading the evidence at the Brantford hearing; he admitted to the truth of the facts as presented. He attempted to minimize the importance of the second stab wound, and implied that it was all part of the same transaction: the second blow had 'followed the first instantly.'[11] He also pointed out that Digges had not been running away but had simply turned around. There was no firm evidence that he was in flight when he received the second wound. Touching briefly on the question of evidence, Freeman cited Upper Canada's 1833 Fugitive Offenders' Act. Harrison spoke up and pointed out that this act had been repealed in the last legislative session. Very well, retorted an embarrassed Freeman, whether or not it had been repealed 'did not touch the question he had raised.'[12] The case for the defence was not off to a promising start.

Freeman quickly came to the heart of his argument. Digges was attempting to return Anderson to slavery, to reduce him to the status of a brute. In these circumstances any person was justified in resisting arrest, even to the extent of killing his captor. Freeman concluded that the homicide was justifiable and extradition could not be ordered.

The only possible flaw in his argument was whether Digges's act in arresting Anderson was a valid one. That is, could a Canadian court recognize the validity of the slave laws of Missouri? It was on this issue of 'double criminality' that Anderson's fate hung. If the arrest by Digges was considered valid in Canada, then Anderson's violent resistance to arrest could render him extraditable. Freeman denied that the Missouri slave laws had any validity in Canada. He maintained that the 'acts must be criminal according to the laws, or the spirit of the laws, of both countries.' Furthermore, the evidence of these criminal acts must be persuasive enough to 'sustain the charge according to the laws of this province.' Arguing that the provincial act set a high standard for the Crown to meet, Freeman suggested that the evidence must be so clear and so overwhelming as to sustain a conviction by Canadian law.[13]

Moreover, it was unthinkable that the Missouri slave laws could be applied in Canada. Freeman cited the *Creole* case, in which the slaves on an American ship had mutinied, killed a man, and sailed to British territory. Lord Denman, speaking in the House of Lords, had declared that '[until] the laws in each country were such as a christian country ought to adopt they could not be enforced by one another.'[14] As a result, the mutineers were not extradited. Freeman argued that the *Creole* case set the standard for the construction of the treaty. It was never the intention of the contracting parties that Britain would have to enforce an unjust law. But Freeman should have been wary of this argument. Shortly after the *Creole* case Britain signed the Webster-Ashburton treaty, a contract with all of the United States, including the slave states. Obviously, if Britain was willing to enter into extradition agreements with countries that fostered slavery, it must expect that one day slaves would be the subject of criminal extradition proceedings. The very signing of the treaty could be seen as a repudiation of the *Creole* decision.

Ultimately, Freeman's case rested on the British abhorrence of slavery. He felt that the court had a duty to consider 'the horrors and degredation of slavery.' Furthermore, 'the construction contended for by the claimants of this prisoner would be enforcing this unjust law.' Because slavery was unjust and unnatural, Digges had no lawful authority to try and detain Anderson; therefore, 'according to our laws Digges' acts were unlawful, and his acts, as well as the prisoner's must be judged by our laws.' Freeman's entire case was reduced to the argument that slave laws were an offence against God, and that Anderson had a legal right to take any measure to effect his escape.

Underlying Freeman' argument was an appeal to something much higher than mere treaties or statutes. He was making a plea for the application of natural law, for universal principles of human dignity that transcended local laws. In Freeman's time men still believed that there were eternal principles that should guide their actions. Sir William Blackstone, the author of the *Commentaries*, had written of the mysterious symmetry between the universal law and the law of England. As a result of Blackstone's writings there was still a strong undercurrent of natural-law thinking in jurisprudence. Because laws 'derived their compulsive force from the laws of nature, it was important to recognize that where an individual saw an ostensible law to be a violation of God's prescriptions, he was obliged to disobey it.'[15] This was precisely the philosophy Freeman was espousing when he paraphrased Lord Denman's argument that 'any act of a slave in asserting his liberty would not be considered an offence to be punished, but rather an act to be approved.'[16] Surely, argued Freeman, the most compelling universal principle was freedom, and Anderson had been breaking no law of nature by striking out for his liberty.

On the whole, Freeman's performance was not very effective. He had chosen to trust his client's life to succeeding on this one issue: because slavery was a violation of natural law, any criminal act done by a slave escaping from slavery was not an offence within the terms of the treaty. Freeman should have taken into account the fact that judges are poor interpreters of divine intent. It is far easier for them to base their decisions on statutes or precedent than on philosophical notions.

Speaking in an almost apologetic tone, Henry Eccles led off the case for the Crown. The government was anxious that the prisoner 'should have the benefit of any doubt, and they desire not to press the case against him in the slightest.' If there was any doubt, Eccles would be pleased to see the prisoner released immediately. Nevertheless, it was his duty as counsel to dissent from Freeman's argument. Eccles went directly to the question of double criminality and pointed out that the treaty was 'to be construed as a contract, and we cannot add exceptions or provisions which it does not contain.' Adding an exemption for acts committed by slaves in the course of escaping would be, in effect, a judicial alteration of the treaty. It was essential to recall that Seneca Digges was empowered by Missouri law to seize and hold the runaway: 'The deceased *had authority*, and upon that distinction the whole question turns.'[17] To this extent, at least, the slave laws of Missouri had to be recognized. John Anderson had killed a man who was lawfully trying to detain him, and on that fact he must be returned.

Finally, Robert Harrison rose to complete the Crown's submission. He also began in an accommodating manner, conceding that he agreed 'with many of the propositions laid down by the counsel for the prisoner.' But his meticulously researched argument would succeed in demolishing Freeman's dramatic appeal to the emotions. The issue was not slavery, Harrison argued, but murder. A temperate examination of the issue would show not only that Canadian courts could examine the slave laws 'but that under the treaty we are *bound* to do so.'[18] For authority Harrison cited the English case of *Mure* v. *Kaye* and Justice Heath's argument that 'crime is inseparable from locality.'[19] To determine whether extradition should be ordered, it was essential to examine the laws of the place where the act was committed. Of course, Canadian evidentiary standards should be applied to ensure that the extradition request was not a sham.

But Harrison cautioned that the courts should not confuse rules of evidence with a plea that Canadian morality and anti-slavery sentiments be applied to a crime committed in a slave state.

Harrison also pointed out that British law gave limited recognition to slavery. In a number of cases British courts had considered slave laws and had found them to be legitimate in their jurisdiction. It was essential, if the treaty was to be effective, that recognition be given to the *lex loci* – the law of the place where the act was committed. Missouri law empowered Digges to arrest Anderson, and the court must recognize this fact. Harrison quoted from *Russell on Crimes*, a text used in both Britain and America: 'Where persons having authority to arrest or imprison, using the proper means for that purpose, are resisted in so doing, and killed, *it will be murder*.'[20] By way of illustration Harrison pointed out that Canadian law provided for imprisonment for debt. Suppose a debtor killed his jailer and escaped to one of the United States that had abolished imprisonment for debt. Could that state, merely because it had no debtors' prisons, refuse to return the killer? Such a conclusion would be outrageous. It followed, then, that 'to kill when in lawful custody is the crime of murder in each country. We have no right to go into the question of the laws which make that custody lawful.'[21]

Harrison also denied Freeman's assertion that a high standard of proof existed. The magistrate was empowered only to investigate the charge, not to try the case. The Brantford investigation had disclosed that Anderson had stabbed the hapless Digges 'as he lay on his face ... Anderson *again* stabbed him – this time in the back.' This was clearly an excess of force, and on this basis alone extradition was justified. '*Prima facie* Anderson is a murderer,' concluded Harrison, but it was up to a Missouri jury to determine the extent of his guilt. If there was any fault here, it lay in the treaty's failure to provide an exemption for escaped slaves. He brought the court back to the inescapable conclusion: 'We have to deal with the treaty as we find it, not as we think it ought to be.'[22] Because the treaty provided no exemption for fugitive slaves, the court had no authority to create an exemption.

It was a masterly performance. Harrison had given a lucid, erudite explanation of the nature of the treaty and the legal obligations arising from it. His brilliant summation had more than justified Macdonald's confidence. From another perspective, however, it might have been to the government's advantage to present a weak case and let the court release Anderson. Life would be much easier if the judges would seize the initiative, free the prisoner, and relieve the administration of its embarrassing obligations. Robert Harrison's thorough exposition had made it all the more likely that Anderson's case would be returned to the ministry for their decision.

With the legal argument complete, Samuel Freeman stood up to make one more request of the court. His client had dictated a statement, and Freeman wished to read it to the judges. So far the court had heard only convoluted legal arguments; it was unusual, but refreshing, when the prisoner made his own statement. Anderson generally affirmed the Crown's case, but added that he had been attacked by club-wielding slaves and that Digges had ordered the slaves to kill him. 'When I started I made up my mind no man should take me alive,' Anderson said. He insisted that he had no apology to make: 'I was compelled to do what I did.'[23]

Chief Justice Robinson set a date for the decision, and adjourned the court. Samuel Freeman appeared to be confident that his client would be released, and it was reported that he had 'no doubt of a favourable result.'[24] The *Globe* felt that 'the Court ... [would] find reason to order his discharge. To an unsophisticated mind, the case scarcely admits of doubt.'[25] This confidence was neither universal nor justified. While there was widespread sympathy for Anderson's plight throughout the province, there was also a determination that the law would be carried out. The *Toronto Leader* expressed this attitude: 'A slave is not authorized to commit murder; and if Jones [as Anderson was still frequently called] be guilty of the crime charged against him, we can see nothing in the *Ashburton* treaty to exempt him from extradition.'[26] The *Ottawa Citizen* was more blunt; it ridiculed Freeman's argument that 'free soil makes free men,' and said that the argument should go further to show that 'a slave guilty of murder in Missouri is free from the consequence of that crime the moment he touches Canadian soil. Surely a proposition so monstrous as this cannot be sustained.'[27] Others openly advocated Anderson's extradition. According to the *Norfolk Messenger*, Anderson had murdered a man and the treaty demanded his return: 'If this be the law it must be admitted and acted upon by the Executive. No other course is open.'[28]

Samuel Freeman was criticized for his handling of the case. The *Leader* was 'afraid that Mr Freeman has somewhat bungled the case of the prisoner.'[29] The newspaper pointed out that he appeared to be unaware that there were two modes of proceeding on habeas corpus. He could have asked the court to quash the writ for insufficiency or for permission to 'plead to the record.' The first method, the one chosen by Freeman, was an all-or-nothing request for release. The second method allowed counsel to raise technical objections to the incarceration, and also provided for an appeal. Freeman's lack of familiarity with this area of law might cost his client his life.

The chief justice had originally scheduled Thursday, 29 November, as the day of judgment. On that morning a large crowd, with 'white and black being mingled together in most admirable confusion,' assembled at Osgoode Hall to hear the decision. There was much anxiety about Anderson's fate, and rumours were about that he would be seized by the mob and spirited into hiding if the judges authorized his extradition. Extra precautions were taken. The night shift of police was ordered to remain on duty and was massed at police headquarters; the officers were ready to storm Osgoode Hall if the prisoner was seized.[30] All the excitement went for naught when the chief justice announced that although he had prepared his decision, his fellow judges Burns and McLean were not yet ready. Despite the tension, Anderson and his police escort returned to jail without incident, and judgment was deferred for two weeks. Rumours circulated that the chief justice was in favour of extradition, or, as the *Globe* expressed it so vividly, 'that [Anderson] ought to be sent back to Missouri *to be burnt alive* by the authorities of Howard country as a terror to all others who may be panting for the liberty that Jones so bravely won and thought he could maintain.'[31] An uneasy shudder went through abolitionist circles when they began to acknowledge that Anderson might be extradited after all.

Excitement and indignation over the Anderson case were now at a peak. The columns of the *Globe* were filled with letters protesting Anderson's ordeal and offering helpful tidbits of constitutional law which might secure his release. One letter writer felt that 'the fate of Anderson is the general topic of conversation,' and added ominously, 'Should Anderson be given up, there will be such a burst of indignation as was never before heard in Canada.' It began to seem as if John Anderson was a martyr to the cause of reform itself. Almost daily the *Globe* published editorials condemning Macdonald and the government for their handling of the case. The question was simple: 'Was [Canada's extradition statute] meant to make Canada the hunting-ground of Southern slave-catchers, and our magistrates, courts, and governors the agents, the gaolers, the blood-hounds of the slave-master?'[32]

In rising to Anderson's defence, the *Globe* also pointed out weaknesses in the case against him. The evidence of a second stab wound came from the hazy recollections of a little boy. There had been no post mortem examination to determine whether such a wound ever existed. These are all valid criticisms, none of which Freeman had raised on behalf of his client. But the *Globe's* case in favour of Anderson ultimately came down to an emotional hatred of slavery.

Suppose a slave woman – young, beautiful, virtuous, and there are many such – assaulted by a white man, her master if you will, with intent to ravish her. She resists, and kills her ravisher ... Suppose this woman has escaped to Canada, and is demanded under the Treaty. Must she be given up? Yes, says Mr Attorney General Macdonald, and yes, says his Toronto organ! We say *No!* – a thousand times *No!!*[33]

When reminded by a law student that judges were required to apply the law as it existed, whatever the consequences, the *Globe* printed a rejoinder. 'Small lawyers and unfinished students-at-law may sneer at newspaper opinions,' but the righteous *Globe* appealed to 'higher notions' of law, and by those notions Anderson was innocent. Slavery was a violation of God's law, thundered the *Globe*, and Anderson was justified in resisting it, 'even unto death.'[34]

The *Globe* even saw something sinister in the government's recent repeal of the 1833 Fugitive Offenders' Act. The suggestion for repeal had come from Colonel Prince of Sandwich, who pointed out that there were two extradition acts in the statute book –the 1833 act, and the 1849 act, which had implemented the Webster-Ashburton treaty in the province.[35] In border constituencies such as the colonel's, this frequently led to confusion. The statute-book was cleaned up, and the 1833 act was repealed.[36] In this innocuous act the *Globe* found evidence of yet a 'deeper and blacker plot' and wondered, 'Did Mr Mathews find that it [the 1833 act] stood in his way?' The ministry gave no reason for the repeal: 'Was it, we ask again, at the suggestion of his slave-catching "henchmen"?'[37] This was ludicrous. At the time, the *Globe* had reported the repeal of the act with no hint of disapproval.[38] The 1849 act did nothing to alter the requirement that the governor general decide the question of extradition. Nevertheless, the *Globe* recklessly advised its readers that 'it was deemed necessary, before commencing this new *slave-trade*, to repeal it out of the way!' It was a measure of the *Globe's* cavalier attitude to the truth that it refused to publish Robert Harrison's correction of the facts. Harrison had to turn to the *Leader* to publish a statement that the 1860 act was intended merely to remove an 'effete and useless' act from the statute-books.[39] Even reform newspapers thought that the *Globe's* attempt to infer a sinister plot from the 1860 act was ludicrous.[40]

In the following days Reformers throughout Canada West seized upon the Anderson case as a likely vehicle to attack the government. In his notes for a speech to be given at a Reform dinner at Fergus, Thomas D'Arcy McGee obliquely referred to the Anderson case when he accused Macdonald of appealing to 'the prejudices of the prejudiced (on subjects of race and religion).'[41] In Simcoe, Michael Foley, one of the few Reformers to stand up to George Brown, made a lengthy speech 'violently attacking Attorney General Macdonald for his conduct in the case.'[42] George Brown did not comment publicly on the affair, and in the second week of December he left for New York. Yet even in Brown's absence there seemed to be a renewed vitality in the *Globe*'s editorials. Macdonald's government was viciously dismissed as representing 'six years of infamy, including every crime known to the political calendar except overt treason.'[43] If the *Globe* could not hold up Macdonald as a traitor, editorial after editorial could flay him as an agent of the slave-catchers.

Contemporaneous with the Anderson case, the provincial newspapers were reporting and enthusiastically applauding Garibaldi's overthrow of the Papal States. One commentator even compared Anderson to Garibaldi, the difference being the harshness of the tyranny they opposed: 'Yet the tyranny of a Bomba, or of a Pope, infamous as it is, is mildness and goodness itself compared with that of those Missourians.'[44] In the imagination of many Canadians Anderson had become a black Garibaldi, struggling for freedom against not only the southern slave-catchers but also their Canadian accomplices, William Mathews and John A. Macdonald.

The Reformers had found an issue with which to harass the administration, but the government's defenders were not idle. The *Hamilton Spectator* maintained that the attorney general was prosecuting the law as he was bound to do. It dismissed the *Globe*'s criticisms: 'One might as soon have expected to hear of Niagara Falls reversing their course, as the Grit organ approving of anything the Attorney General does.' According to the *Spectator*, the opposition was only trying to turn Anderson into an object of political trade. Predictably, William Mathews was enraged by the criticism, and he suggested in a letter published in the *Spectator* that George Brown's only concern in the Anderson case was in 'securing a few more black votes for the next general election.' Furthermore, 'the Editor-in-Chief cares as little for Anderson, and those of his race and color, as he does for his white slaves at Bothwell – his treatment of whom, I have heard, will compare favorably with that of the Missouri slaveholder.'[45] This was pure spite. There was no reason to believe that George Brown's treatment of the employees at his farming enterprise at Bothwell,

Kent County, was any more tyrannical than that of other employers of the period.

The ministry had to do more than merely answer the reformers' taunts. The opposition's disarray in the early part of the year seemed to be giving way to unity as they confronted the government on many issues. The Cartier-Macdonald ministry was already embarrassed by the contretemps over the Prince of Wales' refusal to pass under the Orange arches. Orangemen tended to blame Macdonald for the embarrassment to their order, and to clear up misunderstandings Macdonald decided to embark on a public speaking tour. In the pre-Confederation period there was no province-wide political organization, and it fell to the leader to show himself to his supporters and to prove to the press that a united party existed not only in Parliament but among its followers in the constituencies. Macdonald was convinced that without his leadership the Liberal-Conservatives would degenerate into antagonistic factions. His strong sense of self-value convinced him that without him, the party would still be in the wilderness, 'where they were when I took them up in 1854.'[46] Now his leadership was threatened, for it appeared that a former tory leader, John Hillyard Cameron, would use his position as grand master of the Orange Lodges to form an anti-Macdonald faction within the Liberal-Conservatives. A public speaking tour would bolster Macdonald's leadership, and would demonstrate that a united party existed throughout the province.

Beginning on 9 November 1860, Macdonald toured through Brantford, St Thomas, London, and Hamilton. At all these stops Macdonald was the principal speaker, the voice of the government. Finally, in St Catharines on 3 December, he confronted the *Globe*'s captious critics of the Anderson case. In a lengthy address Macdonald told the faithful that he was merely following the requirements of the extradition laws. It was the government that had ensured that the fugitive would receive all his rights at no expense. 'Strange to say, however, Mr Brown of the *Globe*, attempts to make it a matter of political capital against me, *that instead of sending the man to be tried in the States ... and I had the power to send him at once to Missouri – I sent the matter to the judges, to have it fully decided whether a case was fully made out against him.*'[47] Macdonald even advanced a disingenuous argument that Anderson would be better off being 'tried by the *Magna Charta*, by the law of the land, by a loyal tribunal, than have his case decided by any Cabinet whatever.' This was a startling suggestion; as the attorney general was well aware, the obligation to decide the question of extradition lay squarely with the executive, not with the courts. His remark may have been poor law but it was excellent politics, and the crowd cheered as Macdonald argued that Canada's impartial judiciary should decide the matter. The attorney general was now in full flight, and he proceeded to tell his audience that Conservatives, not Reformers, had been in the forefront of the anti-slavery struggle. It had been Pitt and Wilberforce who had first led the fight against slavery in the British House of Commons. Conservatives could leave the St Catharines meeting reassured of their leader's ability and of the liberality of his policies.

Government newspapers rallied to the ministry. 'The Atty. General very properly referred the matter to the Judges,' noted the *London Free Press*.[48] Even one notable opposition journal, the *Brantford Expositor*, held that the attorney general had acted properly by directing a habeas corpus and that 'this is doubtless the proper course to pursue.'[49] The one relentless source of criticism was the *Globe*. Macdonald's speaking tour was described as 'gatherings of office-holders and office-seekers, of violent Tories, and money-hunting Reformers.' The attorney general's known fondness for strong drink was also touched on. Reporters observed that Macdonald had 'staggered to his hotel in very questionable company at very unseasonable hours.'[50] Macdonald was described as having been too 'exhausted' at one dinner to give his usual speech; the *Globe* commented, '*In vino veritas.*' In a rejoinder to the St Catharines speech, the *Globe* repeated its accusations that 'the Governor, under the advice of his Attorney General, not the Judges, must order the surrender of Anderson.' The *Globe* correctly pointed out that the primary duty was on the ministry to 'consider the policy, the humanity, the "doubts" of his case,' a duty they had deliberately sidestepped.[51]

Americans had followed the proceedings at Osgoode Hall with great interest. Newspapers throughout the states carried reports of the case and the *New York Times* even had a correspondent in the courtroom. The *Times* reporter felt that the case would have a serious bearing 'upon international law, and even as to the relations between Great Britain and the United States.' In an astute evaluation of Macdonald's motives, the reporter concluded that the case had been referred to the courts 'to shield [the government] from responsibility as well as to be sure of correct action.'[52]

American newspaper readers were inured to stories about fugitives. Ever since the passage of the Fugitive Slave Act in 1850 the free states had seen a regular parade of extradition cases. At the time the Anderson case was being argued in Toronto, the city of Cleveland was following the case of the fugitive slave Lucy Bagby. Her former owner had tracked her down and was on the verge of taking her back to the south. She brought a habeas corpus application on the basis that escaping from slavery was not a crime in Ohio and therefore her imprisonment was illegal. During her hearing sympathetic blacks stormed the courthouse in an unsuccessful attempt to free her. Before the rescuers were driven back, snuff and pepper were thrown in her captor's faces. The *Cleveland Leader* condemned her re-enslavement, but urged the blacks to submit to this 'justice-defying' law.[53] In another Ohio case, the state of Kentucky demanded the return of a white man accused of breaking the slave laws by helping slaves to escape. The governor of Ohio, William Dennison, refused on the basis that an extraditable offence also had to be a crime under Ohio law, and it was no crime in Ohio to help a slave to escape. The Ohio decision was, according to the *Globe*, an 'able vindication of international rights and the principles of natural justice ... The Ohio rendition case suggests a contrast not all honourable to the Attorney General of Upper Canada.'[54] Yet the Anderson case overshadowed these incidents; if Anderson was returned, the fugitives would have lost their last North American refuge. The American abolitionist Lewis Tappan grasped the significance of the Anderson case when he told readers of the *Globe* in a published letter that 'the case of Anderson is most important,' for the British government was 'emphatically now the principal asylum of the oppressed.'[55]

Northern abolitionists supported Anderson not only because his case had become a cause célèbre, but because of the threat it posed to Canada as the ultimate haven. The legendary underground railroad had enabled thousands of slaves to escape, to travel through the free states, and to find sanctuary in Canada. A Detroit newspaper feared that 'if this case is decided in favor of the claimants, it will virtually break up the underground railroad, and make Canada no longer a resort for runaways.'[56] One influential newspaper, the *New York Daily Tribune*, emphatically supported the fugitive. In an article that was reprinted throughout the free states, the *Tribune* described the sympathy for Anderson that pervaded Canada. Nevertheless, on a strict reading of the law, it feared, he would be extradited. The *Tribune* counselled vigilant abolitionists in Michigan and New York to watch the border, seize Anderson if he should appear, and give his Missouri captors a ride on 'that celebrated rail of Uncle Abe's.'[57] One American abolitionist, Gerrit Smith of New York, was active in whipping up support for the fugitive. Smith belonged to the 'Free Soil' party, the politically active wing of American abolitionism. The party was violently opposed by William Lloyd Garrison and his followers, who abhorred political activism and linked the anti-slavery cause with other movements such as pacifism and women's rights. Because their enemy Smith sedulously fostered Anderson's cause, the Garrisonians all but ignored it. Their newspaper, the *Liberator*, gave only a perfunctory report of the case.[58]

Of far greater consequence than this split among the abolitionists was the cleavage in American opinions between north and south. Southerners spared little sympathy for Anderson, and expected him to be returned as a matter of course. A Tennessee newspaper saw the case as especially important to those persons 'who lose their negroes.'[59] The extradition treaty could prove useful in regaining lost chattels, for all an owner needed to do was show that the slave had stolen the clothes he was wearing. Another southern newspaper, the *Baltimore American*, was shocked that the *New York Daily Tribune* would actually encourage northerners to free a wanted criminal: 'We trust that the people of Northern New York and Michigan are not so thoroughly blind to all sense of justice as to pay any heed to this most infamous suggestion.' The *American* felt that the killing of Digges was a deliberate act that mandated extradition. Southerners were looking to the Anderson case as a measure of Canadian good faith. 'When such deeds go unpunished, who will say that the people of the South have no cause of complaint.'[60]

Americans, both northerners and southerners, thought that the treaty would inevitably result in Anderson's extradition, for a refusal to return the fugitive would be seen as a breach of the treaty's obligations. The *New York Times* correspondent wrote that Attorney General Macdonald feared that the case could be 'a ca[u]sus belli between the two countries.'[61] In normal times the Anderson affair might have been, if not a cause of war, at least a very sore point between Britain and America. These were not normal times.

On 20 December 1860 South Carolina hoisted the Palmetto flag and seceded from the Union. The greatest crisis in the history of the American republic was about to divert attention away from the fate of one black man.

6

'The Wrangling Courts and Stubborn Law'

The judges who presided over the Anderson case – Sir John Beverley Robinson, Archibald McLean, and Robert Easton Burns – were remembered by one lawyer as 'great jurists in whose honour and learning any litigant might well have the fullest confidence.'[1] This confidence was by no means universally accepted, and was about to be sternly tested.

There was a remarkable similarity in the origins and attitudes of the members of the province's judiciary. In the colony's earliest years the judges were often English appointees who sojourned only long enough to secure a more prestigious position elsewhere. After 1830 Canadian judges tended to be native sons whose future lay in the province. The men who populated the benches seemed to be cast from a single mould. Almost all of them were the sons of loyalists. They had received a proper tory education at Dr John Strachan's grammar school. Most of them served in the War of 1812. Later, in government, they tended to support the tory faction.[2]

Because they had been so identified as a part of the previous tory administrations, the judges were frequently the objects of reformer attacks. In 1845 the *Globe* had launched a vicious assault on Justice McLean: 'The feeling is strong in Upper Canada, that *no Reformer is safe to go with a case, in any degree political, before the Judges, –* and Mr McLean's recent behaviour will strengthen the feeling *– and justly so.*' McLean's great offence had been to omit the name of the provincial administrator at the toasts given at the annual St Andrew's dinner. For this slight to a reformer, the *Globe* mordantly condemned him as a 'jack-daw chucked by the merest accident into a station which he never was, and never will be fit to fill.'[3] Two years later the *Globe* complained that not even the bench of justice was sacred. No confidence could be placed in the judges, for 'we are now to hold our lives and properties at the will of irresponsible uncontrolled judges.'[4]

When the courts ruled in favour of reformers, however, the *Globe* could be effusive in its praise. George Brown was accused in 1857 of having libelled Dr Workman, the medical superintendent of Toronto's lunatic asylum. In his charge to the jury Chief Justice Robinson urged them to respect the freedom of the press.[5] The jury reached a deadlock, the suit was dropped, and Brown declared victory. This great triumph for liberty he attributed at least partially to 'the eminence of the presiding judge,' whose charge to the jury 'was all that could be desired.' In another highly political case, the 'Norfolk Shrievalty' scandal of 1859, the reformers were forced to concede that the courts had rendered an unbiased decision. John Macdonald had appointed a party stalwart, Lawrence W. Mercer, to a vacancy as sheriff of Norfolk County. It later turned out that Mercer had arranged to purchase the resignation of the previous sheriff. Mercer was charged with illegally buying public office, and Macdonald's administration was accused of 'the sale of offices to help [their] friends.'[6] At the trial the prosecution, led by Robert Harrison, argued that a three-century-old criminal statute (5 & 6 Edw. vi, c. 16) prohibited 'corruption' in the sale of public offices. The defence argued that this venerable act was not one of general application and therefore had not been adopted as part of Canadian law. This was a plausible defence, and it might have enabled the Court's conservative majority, Robinson and McLean, to acquit Mercer. But to the embarrassment of the administration, they ruled against the prisoner.[7] The *Asylum Libel* and *Mercer* cases had shown that the Court of Queen's Bench was no servile adjunct of the Cartier-Macdonald administration.

Nevertheless, the one major political trial of the era had forever soured the reformers on the judiciary. Only two years before the Anderson case the Canadian courts had been called on to decide an issue which had all the dimensions of a state trial. The case arose out of the parliamentary confrontation of 1858. After Macdonald and Cartier were defeated in a vote of confidence, George Brown tried to form an administration. Upon taking office, his ministers were required by law to resign and seek election. When Brown returned to the House his ministry was defeated, and he asked for a dissolution. The governor general refused, and Cartier and Macdonald again formed the government. They neatly avoided having to resign their seats by applying the provisions of the Independence of Parliament Act. That act specified that so long as a minister assumed a different post from the one he had resigned from a month before, he did not have to seek re-election. The members of the new Cartier-Macdonald ministry were sworn into one set of offices, resigned from them, and were at once sworn back into the offices that they had held before Brown's ministry had interrupted their affairs.[8]

This 'double shuffle' outraged Brown, and he brought legal actions to have the courts of Queen's Bench and Common Pleas declare that Macdonald and some of his ministers were illegally in Parliament. There was no doubt that the government had violated the spirit of the act. However, there was no violation of the strict words of the statute, and the lawsuits were dismissed. Brown had argued that the courts should look at the intention of the legislature when they passed the act. Yet the rule of construction was and is that the judges must interpret the words of the statute and may adjust or add to the wording only if a strict interpretation would lead to a contradictory or absurd result. All five judges who heard the lawsuits – even a known reformer, Justice W.B. Richards – agreed that technically there had been no violation of the law. The chief justice of Common Pleas, William Henry Draper, ruled that political reasons undoubtedly played a role, 'but these are not judicial reasons, and they never have, as yet, at any time, been referred to, to assist in construing an act of Parliament.' The 'double shuffle' cases presented no great difficulty for the judges. They could not consider politics in their decision, and it was clear that the ministry's acts were within the letter of the law.

Nevertheless, a furious George Brown thundered in the columns of the *Globe* that 'there is not even a pretence of independence' in the judges' decision. 'Can anything be conceived in the shape of decisions more closely resembling partizanship than those now before us?' he asked. Most of Brown's rage was reserved for Chief Justice Draper. 'Mr Draper has mistaken the place and age. He would have made a very fair Jeffreys, and might have served even for the Bloody Assizes.'[9]

Thus, in the years before the Anderson case, Canadian judges were subject to the accusation that they were politicians on leave. Some idea of popular notions of the political character of judges can even be gleaned from Macdonald's St Catharines speech. According to the attorney general, the judges were beyond reproach, for no honest reformer would dare to 'cast a stain on the ermine of Sir John Robinson.' Significantly, Macdonald insisted on calling Robinson a 'Conservative Judge' and assured his listeners that 'no Conservative will breathe a word against Mr Justice Richards or the other Reformers on the Bench.'[10] To his mind, and probably to the minds of most people, the presiding judges could be neatly categorized according to their politics.

Yet the judges do not seem to have acted in a partisan manner. Confronted with political situations, they chose to act independently from the administration and rigorously followed Blackstone's dictum to apply the existing law. If the judges remained true to this pattern they would have to ignore the emotional debate concerning the morality of slavery that raged in their courtroom. They might have to apply the letter of the law to the detriment of real justice.

On the judgment day, 15 December 1860, fifty Toronto policemen, the bulk of the force, were called out to prevent any attempt by sympathizers to free Anderson. Twenty of the policemen were armed with muskets and fixed bayonets, which they stacked neatly on the lawn outside Osgoode Hall. The police were a tangible warning that, if necessary, armed force would uphold the law. As further insurance, a company of soldiers of the Royal Canadian Rifles were stationed a mere five-minute march away at Government House. For the first time since the Rebellion of 1837, the courts at Osgoode Hall bore the appearance of an armed camp.[11]

Many of Toronto's black citizens, and a good number of its white ones, jammed into the court precincts. To control this crowd, estimated at about two hundred persons, Sheriff Jarvis had ordered that only lawyers should be given tickets for the few seats available in the courtroom. When the doors were opened at ten, however, a number of Anderson's black friends managed to elude police and squeeze into the courtroom. J.E. Farewell, a young Toronto law clerk, recalled the excitement the Anderson case caused in the city. All of his fellow clerks discovered that they had agency work to do at Osgoode Hall and joined the crowd at the courthouse.

The day in which judgment was given was one not to be forgotten. It was generally understood that the coloured people intended to use force to prevent Anderson's extradition. The courtroom was packed with coloured men, also the space between the walls and the railing surrounding the rotunda, the stairs, the ground floor and the grounds outside the Hall. A visitor at the Hall would have been surprised to see that nearly every regular policeman and many specials, with rifles and fixed bayonets, were stationed in the court-room in and around the approaches to the stairs.[12]

Most of the crowd could not even get into Osgoode Hall, and one curbside orator took advantage of the ready-made audience to plead for votes for the Liberal party. The liberals would be just to the coloured people, he said and he urged the 'fair ones' in the crowd 'not to lavish tender caresses upon their loved ones until they had voted for Cameron for Mayor.' The crowd hooted him off the street.

By 10:15 the courtroom was full and the spectators were waiting eagerly for the arrival of the judges. A few minutes later their lordships filed in, and the chief justice asked Sheriff Jarvis to produce the prisoner. An embarrassed sheriff approached the bench and explained that owing to a misunderstanding Anderson was still in jail and could not be brought up until noon. Acting as if this were merely another case, the chief justice set it aside and the court dealt with a number of commercial matters. The onlookers quickly became bored and left the court to wander the grounds around Osgoode Hall.

Finally at noon, John Anderson was ushered into the prisoner's dock. Excited whispers went through the crowd as the fugitive, bearing a look of 'mildness and intelligence,' was led into court. He paused for a moment and scanned the crowd in search of familiar faces. He then turned to face the judges for their decision.

Chief Justice Robinson meticulously canvassed every item of evidence and every pertinent clause of the Webster-Ashburton treaty. He conceded that the warrant was defective in that it failed to specify that Anderson was charged with murder, and that the deponent to the information against him, James Gunning, had not been a witness to the killing. Robinson concluded that 'the ends of justice are not allowed to be defeated by a want of proper form in the warrant.'[13] The chief justice also held that to argue technicalities would have done the prisoner no good. Freeman, 'who argued his case with much zeal and ability,' had not raised these irregularities, and, in the chief's opinion, it would have been futile to do so.

The statute the court had to interpret, the Fugitive Offenders' Act of 1849, had implemented the Webster-Ashburton treaty in Canada.[14] On the issue of double criminality, both the statute and the treaty contained similar wording. Section 1 of the provincial act required that the evidence 'be deemed sufficient by him [the presiding magistrate] to sustain the charge according to the laws of this province if the offence alleged had been committed therein.' The treaty required some evidence of criminality as would justify 'the apprehension of the party and his commitment for trial.' In another part, the treaty required evidence sufficient 'to sustain the charge.' In Robinson's opinion, nothing turned on this variation in expression. A crucial point was at stake here. Did the wording in the treaty mean that the Crown had to prove that Anderson had committed a criminal act in both jurisdictions, or that it had only to show that there was sufficient evidence to put him on trial? To the dismay of the defence, Robinson agreed with the second interpretation, 'since by the treaty evidence sufficient *to commit the party for trial* is all that is required to warrant his being given up. And indeed it would not be reasonable to require more.'[15] The Crown's case had successfully passed a major hurdle.

The central question of the case remained the extent to which the court would recognize the Missouri slave laws. Obviously, the laws in Britain and America would differ in significant ways, but the chief justice noted that evidence of Missouri laws was admissible in British courts. Therefore, the Missouri law that enabled any white man to seize a fugitive had to be recognized in Canada as a valid law in Missouri. To Robinson the one outstanding piece of evidence was the fact that Seneca Digges 'was acting under legal authority as much as if he had been armed with process' at the time he detained Anderson.[16] Anderson had therefore killed a person who was acting with the state's authority, and he was subject to extradition according to the treaty. As to the degree of his guilt, Robinson airily observed that 'it will be for the jury to dispose of the case under the direction of a judge.' He thereby avoided dealing with the reality that upon his return to Missouri John Anderson faced either an impromptu trial and execution or a summary lynching.

The chief justice was not totally unaware of these unpleasant alternatives. But he correctly pointed out that 'that was a consideration to be entertained while the subject of the treaty was under discussion, and before it became a law.' There was simply nothing in the treaty that exempted fugitive slaves from extradition for crimes committed by them while escaping. The law was clear: 'Those who are to act judicially in carrying the statute into effect must, so far as the statute allows, carry out the treaty faithfully. They have no right to decline doing so on account of any distinction or consideration which neither the statute nor the treaty has made the ground of an exception.'[17] Appeals to 'higher notions of law' made no headway with the chief justice. In his view, judges 'are not at liberty to act upon considerations of policy, or even of compassion, where a duty is prescribed.' The chief justice reminded his listeners that this was a political decision, and that the governor general could still refuse to surrender the fugitive.

The next judge to speak, Archibald McLean, was not prepared to wait for the governor general's compassion. McLean had known Robinson for most of their lives. They had fought together through the War of 1812 and the political turmoil of the 1820s. Unlike the chief justice, McLean was a fervent abolitionist, and his decision embodied the passions of the anti-slavery cause. He began by noting the many procedural irregularities in the magistrate's orders. The commitment order was not in conformity with the extradition statute either in form or in substance. Mathews had erroneously drafted the commitment in the form reserved for trials. Obviously, Anderson could not be tried in Canada, and the commitment was therefore void. Moreover, the evidence of William Baker and Thomas Digges consisted mostly of Digges's dying recollections. Although this evidence was usually admissible as an exception to the exclusion of hearsay evidence, McLean held that it was not admissible because there was no proof that Digges was 'in full belief that his life was drawing speedily to a close.' This was stretching the requirements of the hearsay exception to an extreme. In the case of any prisoner other than an escaped slave, Digges's dying description of the incident probably would have been admissible. Justice McLean was redrafting the rules of evidence to suit the case of the prisoner before him.

McLean was even able to dismiss the one conclusive piece of evidence in the Crown's case. Phil's affidavit had proved that Anderson had wielded the knife that killed Seneca Digges. McLean noted with incredulity that the affidavit had been entered into evidence with no objection from the defence. He then observed that the second clause of the Fugitive Offenders' Act stated that affidavits should be used only when they were in support of a warrant. Because Phil's affidavit had not been used to substantiate a Missouri warrant (if such a warrant even existed), McLean ruled it inadmissible in Canada.

Finally, McLean revealed the beliefs that underlay his convictions in favour of Anderson. The prisoner was a fugitive from 'the adjoining republic [where] the evils and the curse of slavery are every day becoming more manifest.' In contrast to Robinson's disinterested review of the facts, McLean held that Digges was pursuing the fugitive 'for the unholy purpose of riveting his chains more securely ... in my judgment the prisoner was justified in using any degree of necessary force to prevent what to him must inevitably have proved a most fearful evil.' For Justice McLean, natural-law principles prevailed. Since slavery was against the law of nature, there was no criminality in resisting it. As he neared the end of his judgment, McLean became more adamant about the righteousness of Anderson's cause and the abolitionist struggle. Missouri's slave laws were 'passed by the strong for enslaving and tyrannising over the weak' and should never be recognized in Canada.[18] In Canada, anyone who protected himself against enslavement acted in self-defence. Therefore, the same defence applied to an act committed in Missouri. This reasoning was based on the premise that the laws of a slave state could never be considered by a Canadian court in an extradition proceeding. In McLean's words, 'In administering the laws of a British province, I can never feel bound to recognize as law any enactment which can convert into chattels a very large number of the human race.'

When McLean finished speaking, a great cheering and stamping of feet resounded in the courtroom. McLean had drawn on the deepest feelings of his hearers, and they responded with noisy approval. After hearing McLean's ringing phrases, Anderson, who had been sitting with stoic calm, brightened up, and his face glowed with pleasure. The chief justice restored order, and the court proceeded with the last judgment. Everything now hung on the opinion of Robert Burns.

Burns was an anomaly among the judges of the period. He had few political connections, and owed his appointment to the bench to his outstanding record as a trial lawyer. He displayed his great ability by giving a lucid and relatively brief decision. The defence's argument was simply that any escaped slave had a right to kill his pursuers. 'That argument is a fallacy,' Burns concluded, 'for the two governments in making the treaty were dealing with each other upon the footing that each had at that time recognised laws applicable to the offences enumerated.'[19] Nowhere did the Webster-Ashburton treaty exempt fugitive slaves from its provisions. He concluded, as had the chief justice, that Digges possessed lawful authority and that by killing him Anderson had defied that authority. Burns cautioned that the court had no power to try Anderson. Their only duty was to see if there was evidence of criminality sufficient to make him face a Missouri jury. That Canada did not tolerate slavery was not grounds for saying, as a proposition of law, that a slave could commit murder while attempting to escape from slavery. There was no 'anti-slavery principle' in the law that protected Anderson. Neither was it true that slaves were excluded from extradition under the Webster-Ashburton treaty.[20] An escaped slave was as much responsible for his actions as any other person. The treaty provided no exceptions. The judges were not so naïve as to overlook what Chief Justice Robinson called 'the understanding or instructions' between Britain and the United States which, for practical purposes, exempted from the treaty acts committed by slaves to effect their escape. But these were political, not legal, matters, and the court could not consider them. As Justice Burns put it:

However much I deplore the necessity of being called on to give any opinion, and however much I may detest and abominate the doctrine that any one portion of the human race has a right to deprive another portion of its liberty, and reduce that class to a state of slavery, yet when called on to explain and interpret an agreement between our own nation and another, and what is the legal effect of it, a duty attaches so sacred that private feelings ought in no manner to be allowed to warp the mind or pervert the judgment ... it would be neither fair nor honest to interpret the treaty by the laws of one of the countries, without reference to the laws of the other as they stood at the time the treaty was entered into.[21]

Immediately after Burns had finished, Freeman announced that his client intended to appeal to the Court of Error and Appeal. The chief justice doubted whether an appeal lay to that court, but offered to give Anderson leave to proceed before any appropriate body.

As Anderson was taken into custody, the significance of the decision slowly became apparent to his supporters. Queen's Bench had concluded that he could not be released, and only an appeal to the governor general could save him. As Anderson was led from Osgoode Hall one black on-looker called out. 'Three cheers for Judge McLean,' and the crowd roared its approval of the judge and prisoner. Outside the court, ranks of police with bayonets at the ready surrounded the prisoner and placed him in a cab. The cortège moved slowly through the crowd and returned to the jail without incident. The troops stationed at the Government House likewise returned to their barracks. The display of police and military power had undoubtedly dissuaded any would-be liberators.

In the days following the decision, Archibald McLean found himself thrust unexpectedly into public notoriety. He received effusive praise from press and pulpit, and was described, almost incoherently, as a 'freedom-loving of a freedom-giving freeman,' whose legal opinion was 'without a flaw.'[22] At public rallies he was referred to as the 'venerable Judge' whose conduct had earned him the highest credit. While McLean was being elevated, his colleagues Robinson and Burns were being pilloried by the press. To the opposition newspapers the majority's decision was a 'disgrace to the British Bench ... we appear to have Taneys instead of Mansfields on the Bench.'[23] The chief justice was accused of having 'labored so to twist the evidence, the facts and the law as to support this foregone conclusion.'[24] As a result of the Anderson case, the courts and the government were scarred by 'imbecility and corruption.' Furthermore, 'the judges have sunk themselves a hundred per cent in public estimation; and faith in the purity of the administration of justice in the high Courts has received a shock it will take years to recover from.'[25]

Other observers were more circumspect. The *Globe* felt that the majority decision did not 'convey the idea of great research, or even of tolerably fair *nisi prius* law.'[26] Archibald McLean was saluted by the *Globe* – a remarkable turnabout from its previous calls for his removal. Forgotten was the praise of Robinson's 'fair and liberal' conduct of the *Asylum Libel* case. In the eyes of the *Globe* editors, yesterday's Solomon quickly became today's Jeffreys.

Most of the province gave a more balanced assessment of the judgment. The *Montreal Pilot* observed that 'the Judges themselves were greatly pained to have come to such a decision, and would gladly, could they have done it conscientiously, given judgment the other way ... But it was their duty to interpret the law, and not make it.'[27] 'The Judges will naturally have to bear a good deal of odium,' said the *Hamilton Spectator*, 'but a little calm reflection will be sufficient to satisfy anyone that they have decided in accordance with law.'[28] The Anderson decision had aroused the sympathy of all British America. One New Brunswick reporter felt that no matter what the law said, 'pure British feeling of love of liberty' would save the fugitive.[29]

In the weeks following the decision, public meetings were arranged to express outrage at Anderson's dilemma. At Toronto's St Lawrence Hall a huge crowd, which included most of the city's Protestant clergy and liberals, gathered to denounce the court's decision. Mayor Adam Wilson opened the meeting, and declared that although he disagreed with the judges he would certainly not attribute any 'unworthy or improper motives to them.' Wilson compared Anderson to Garibaldi and maintained that both men had shed blood for freedom, yet neither were assasins. Scottish-born Professor Daniel Wilson spoke next, and told the crowd that this was a special moment for Canadians. For the first time they were expected to take the lead in the war against slavery: 'The Empire as a whole looks upon us now to see how we shall fulfill that sacred trust that is committed to us.' The boisterous crowd cheered as Wilson extolled Canada, the true home of the free. He best captured the spirit of the moment when he asked the audience to imagine a fleeing Anderson whispering in his wife's ear 'the secret which had dawned on his own soul, that the lone north star pointed to a country beyond the

Lakes where freedom was at length secured to man ... where Divine and moral law was recognized.' The citizens applauded all references to 'freedom' and 'Canada' and hissed all mention of 'Bill Mathews.'

The most passionate speech of the evening was delivered by John Scoble of the Dawn settlement. In 1843 Scoble, then the secretary of the British and Foreign Anti-Slavery Society, had asked the principal British negotiator, Lord Ashburton, whether fugitive slaves were caught up by the extradition treaty. Ashburton told him that Article x was not designed to include fugitive slaves. When Scoble sought assurances from the foreign secretary, Lord Aberdeen, he received an equally vague reply: 'The greatest care would be taken to prevent in their case the abuse of the extradition article.' Ambiguous as these responses were, Scoble announced to the receptive crowd that the weight of the entire British government was on their side. The British government had guaranteed, Scoble declared, that fugitive slaves who committed crimes during the course of escape would not be subject to extradition.[30] Unlike Mayor Wilson, Scoble was leery of the judges, and he warned his listeners that 'the people of England owed their liberties less to Judges than to juries.' Resolutions were then passed declaring that the Webster-Ashburton treaty did not apply to fugitive slaves, and that Anderson should be instantly released.

Rallies of support were held in Anderson's behalf in Montreal, Hamilton, and smaller centres. At a Montreal assembly Thomas D'Arcy McGee compared the lot of the southern slaves to that of the Catholic Irish, and then asked, 'Are we to betray the Edomite though he be our brother?'[31] At the Hamilton rally a Dr Hurlburt suggested that the judges were right and that they were merely applying an unjust law. Was it the purpose of the meeting, he asked, to pressure the judges into making an illegal but popular judgment? All subsequent speakers expressed shock at Hurlburt's question and denounced any view contrary to the prevailing one – that the judges were wrong and that Anderson was a hero.[32]

With relatively few refugee blacks in its midst, Canada East might have been expected to take a detached position. However, one Montreal newspaper, Le Canadien, vociferously supported the fugitive. The newspaper took an early interest in the case and realized that it would affect the extradition laws with the United States. If extradition required the return of escaped slaves to the laws 'sous le nom de juge Lynch' the result would be intolerable, for 'nous n'aimerions pas que cet usage s'introduisit en Canada, fusse pour empêcher les gens d'être pendus ou brûlés. Nous n'aimons le juge Lynch ni dans ses actes de rigueur ni dans ses actes de clémence.' If the price of the Webster-Ashburton treaty was the return of fugitive slaves, then the price was too high. *Le Canadien* also thought that Anderson's case should be decided on principle, not statute – that is, 'en vertu des principes de la loi naturelle et de la justice éternelle' rather than by 'des arguties de la jurisprudence vulgaire.'

After the decision of Queen's Bench was rendered, *Le Canadien* condemned Robinson and Burns as loudly as George Brown's *Globe*: 'Le jugement en question, trouvera la censure bien méritée.'[33] Despite the enthusiasm of *Le Canadien*, there was little interest among French Canadians in Anderson's fate. A Montreal rally in support of Anderson was attended almost exclusively by members of the English-speaking community. A.A. Dorion, Brown's Canada East lieutenant, and Mayor Charles-Séraphin Rodier of Montreal were the only prominent French Canadians present. A better reflection of French Canadian opinions was the clerical publication *La Minerve*. It condemned the Montreal rally as 'dangereux et deplacée' and urged that the law take its course. It serenely urged the abolitionists of Canada West, 'Respecter leurs [the judges'] decisions et s'y soumettre sans murmure.'[34] The English journals of Canada East did more than murmur against the decision of Queen's Bench. To the *Quebec Mercury*, Justice Burns was 'so ignorant of criminal law, and so conscientious in his timidity and subservience, that any opinion he may utter is excusable; but that consummate lawyer, the Chief Justice Sir John Beverley Robinson, has 'sinned with knowledge,' and is a fit and proper subject for impeachment.'[35]

Having been thoroughly despoiled and diminished by the press, the case was in due course brought back to the judges. A week after the hearing, Freeman, now assisted by Matthew Cameron and Thomas Hodgins, asked for and received the court's permission to seek a writ of habeas corpus from the Court of Common Pleas. At that time Canada West possessed two separate courts of common law – Queen's Bench and Common Pleas – as well as a Court of Chancery. The usual practice, as Chief Justice Robinson observed, was for each common law court to uphold the decision of the other. The Anderson case was exceptional, however, and the chief justice thought that Common Pleas would be inclined to give an independent judgment on the case. Anderson was thereby assured of at least two more appeals in Canada as well as an appeal to the Privy Council in England. It was possible that these series of appeals would exhaust the resources of his pursuers. Even though the threat of extradition still hung over John Anderson, his supporters remained hopeful that some way would be found to secure his release. '[That] the judgment will ultimately go in favour of the prisoner we cannot for a moment doubt,' said the *Montreal Pilot*.[36]

The Anderson decision had been a major blow to the public esteem of the Canadian judiciary. In the minds of many people the objectivity of the courts was already highly suspect. The 'double shuffle' case and frequent innuendos had given the impression that the courts were subject to political persuasion. The Anderson case became 'one of those infamous prostitutions of judicial power to political expediency which in this degenerate age have too frequently polluted the judicial ermine.'[37] With no understanding of the legal complexities involved, an American abolitionist, Gerrit Smith, was able to harangue a Toronto crowd and ask why the court had 'descended from the glorious heights of the British law to the dark hell of slavery's law.'[38] Those who criticized the judges so intemperately had no idea of the requirements of the treaty and the clear obligation to return fugitive criminals. When examined against the law and the facts of the case, the court's decision is consistent with its previous rulings. The majority had applied the law *as it was*, not as they would have it. They were obligated to refuse to release Anderson and to direct him to seek relief from the source of the law, the government. In so doing the majority remained aloof from politics and applied the law to the case before them. They judged the nature of the act, not the individual.

Fervid abolitionists could not make these fine distinctions. They were committed to saving an individual, and for them the decision of Queen's Bench was only one battle in an extended war. The struggle for John Anderson's freedom was about to be extended beyond the judges to the politicians. Abolitionists began to mobilize their considerable diplomatic and legal resources. The struggle to save the fugitive was about to pool the resources of the Canadian, American, and British anti-slavery movements.

7

England Intervenes

On the Monday following the decision of Queen's Bench, Thomas Henning, the secretary of the Anti-Slavery Society of Canada, wrote to Louis Alexis Chamerovzow, his counterpart in the British and Foreign Anti-Slavery Society, begging for British help, 'for if Anderson be returned as it is feared he may be, no fugitive will be safe in Canada.'[1] John Scoble had also written to the British society about the court decision. The baton was about to be passed from Canadian to British abolitionists.

The British abolitionists needed Anderson almost as badly as he needed them. Since the imperial emancipation in 1833, the anti-slavery movement in England had become moribund. They could rail against the curse of slavery in the southern states and Latin America, but there was little that British agitation could do to stop it. As well, the bitter divisions that hindered American abolitionism affected the British anti-slavery movement. Yet the petty factionalism that divided abolitionists was becoming more and more irrelevant to an uninterested British public. The anti-slavery movement had become a 'marginal affair' in Britain, largely because there did not exist any issue that could ignite the public interest. The Anderson case was the first real cause the English abolitionists had had to work with in years, and they seized upon it with genuine zeal.[2]

An executive committee meeting of the British and Foreign Anti-Slavery Society was held on 4 January 1861, and Henning's and Scoble's letters were read to the members. The committee authorized a petition to the colonial secretary, the Duke of Newcastle, and Chamerovzow was instructed to arrange a meeting between the duke and an anti-slavery delegation. These resolutions were too tame for Louis Chamerovzow; he was so inflamed by the case that he initiated his own plan to save the fugitive. His zeal in the cause of abolition might have been attributable to his own background.[3] As an expatriate Pole in England, he probably felt himself to be as marginal a member of society as Anderson was in Canada. Neglecting his career as a novelist, Chamerovzow had dedicated himself to the anti-slavery movement, and in 1852 he had succeeded Scoble as secretary of the society. Despite his enthusiasm, however, the movement had foundered owing to public indifference. But the Anderson case had given the anti-slavery movement new life and Chamerovzow a cause. Within days he had got in touch with over 250 individuals and groups, who posted hundreds of memorials to the colonial secretary.[4]

The British press was fascinated by the case, and instantly gave it wide publicity. In denouncing the decision, the newspapers flayed the Canadian judges. This was the kind of chuckle-headed law that might be expected from a colonial court, wrote *Punch*. The 'monstrous opinion' of the majority undoubtedly would be rectified by Lord Brougham and the liberal judges of England. *Punch* even saw something sinister in the judge 'ominously named Burns ... delivering up this mulatto to miscreants who, if they get him, will probably burn him alive with green wood.'[5] At least other newspapers were more civil. According to the *Liverpool Mercury*, the Canadian judges had reached an 'inexplicable conclusion,' and had taken a 'too narrowly technical' view of the case. The written law should defer to natural justice. The Canadian judges were guilty of the grossest misinterpretation, said the *London Post*: 'Are they [fugitive slaves] all to be relegated to the whip and the tortures of the planter because a majority of the Canadian Judges think that the word "murder" in the treaty is to be interpreted according to the laws of Missouri, and not in accordance with the enlightened and humane principles of English freedom?'[6]

Typical of British disdain for the colonial courts was the attitude of a Glasgow newspaper, which condemned the 'want of that solidity and depth of legal learning there which would have been displayed in England, had the matter been argued before our highest Courts.' In contrast, the *Economist* rose to the defence of Robinson and Burns by recognizing that the point at issue had never before been argued in a court. Moreover, the critical question of whose laws should define the offences listed in the treaty had never been addressed by the diplomats in the framing of the treaty. It had been naïvely presumed that the listed offences were so universal in character that there was no need for definition. Still, the *Economist* maintained that the Canadian judges had reached the wrong conclusion. The general intention of the treaty had to be looked at and that intention would have revealed the reluctance of Britain to bind herself to return a fugitive slave, even a slave who had killed his pursuer. This was a weak argument, one (as even the *Economist* conceded) based more on morality and a sense of 'right' than in the law. These cerebral arguments went largely unnoticed by the British public. The editorial in the *London Dial* probably best reflected popular outrage at the prospect of Anderson's extradition: 'If every law in the Canadian Statute Book, and the British Statute Book to boot, together with every line in the Petition of Right and Magna Charta, required the surrender of John Anderson to be burnt alive, the authoritative voice of the British people, rising deep and clear above all written law in the assertion of natural justice, would forbid the deed.'[7] The British press overwhelmingly supported Anderson and found the Canadian decision incomprehensible and positively 'unBritish.' Only the newspapers in Leeds (which were staunchly anti-slavery) were willing to say that the opinion of the Canadian judges was correct in law. The influential *Times* agreed that the judges had interpreted the treaty properly: 'They [decided] no more than that a fugitive who has, in resisting his lawful apprehension, killed an American citizen, and then taken refuge in Canada, must be given up. This cannot be honestly gainsaid.'[8] Regretfully, the *Times* admitted that the Canadian judges had reached the 'right conclusion.'

On the minds of every Englishman was the fate of Count Teleki. Only months before, Saxony had surrendered this Hungarian patriot to the harsh justice of imperial Austria. This surrender had been loudly condemned as a concession to the most villainous tyranny. English newspapers speculated whether 'Saxon law' was about to be applied to Anderson's case. Typically, British outrage at the Anderson decision was mingled with a denunciation of slavery. The *London Despatch*, for example, had only a vague understanding of the facts. Nevertheless, it told its readers that slave laws could not be applied in extradition cases. It was a 'first principle' of law that all men are free, and it therefore followed that 'it is not Anderson, but the Missouri slaveholders who are the violators of this principle.' Having established Anderson's innocence, the editors, in colourful if irrational terms, invited the Americans to seize the fugitive: 'If instead of only the little paltry Province of Missouri, we had to deal with the united force of the great American Confederation, the reply ought still to be "There he is, and touch him if you dare."' An English poet, W.C. Bennett, linked Anderson with that other freedom-lover, Garibaldi, and reminded his readers in verse:

> You who of Garibaldi rave,
>   And howl at Bourbons, chain this slave!
> His right arm struck the self-same blows
>   Italian bondsmen dealt of late.
> With them he's one of slavery's foes.
> Give him to worse than Bomba's hate.[9]

To the British press John Anderson had become a black hero to be shielded at all costs from the demonic 'slavocracy.'

Public indignation was at a high pitch, and the colonial secretary acted quickly to ensure that Anderson remained in British hands. On 9 January 1861 he ordered the acting governor of Canada, Sir William Fenwick Williams, to abstain from completing the extradition, and reminded him that the fugitive's delivery was an administrative and not a judicial function. Newcastle added gratuitously, 'Her Majesty's Government are not satisfied that the decision of the Court at Toronto is in conformity with the view of the Treaty which has hitherto guided the authorities in this country.'[10] The foreign secretary, Lord John Russell, was also convinced that the Canadians were wrong. Russell had met Chief Justice Robinson during the Canada Bill debate of 1839, when Robinson had represented the conservative element in Canada and Russell the liberal administration of Lord Melbourne. Russell retained bitter memories of those days. He wrote to Newcastle, 'I believe the law is against Chief Justice Robinson but he cannot bear liberty in any form.'[11] The leaders of the British government were prepared to believe, without seriously examining the issue, that the Canadians were wrong.

Each of the two organizations dedicated to John Anderson's welfare, the Colonial Office and the British and Foreign Anti-Slavery Society, operated in ignorance of what the other was about to do. The day before Newcastle sent his instructions to Canada, Chamerovzow had expressed his concern that the colonial secretary would not stop Anderson's return because he would be afraid to interfere 'with the prerogatives of the Canadian courts.'[12] On 10 January Chamerovzow received a letter from a lawyer, Frederick Solly Flood, suggesting that the society try to obtain a writ of habeas corpus in England. Seizing upon this idea, Chamerovzow instructed Flood and a solicitor to begin proceedings. The usually slow-moving judicial system acted with breathtaking speed, and a hearing was scheduled to take place five days after the lawyers first held their strategy session. The day before the hearing Chamerovzow had an offer of help from two more barristers, Gordon Allen and a colourful member of Parliament, Edwin James, QC. The lawyers decided that James would conduct the case assisted by Allen and Flood. On the day of the hearing they were joined by another barrister, George Denman. All of this had been arranged without instructions from the society: one day before the hearing the society's executive committee met and retroactively sanctioned the acts of their impetuous secretary.[13] Instead of preaching abstract sermons on the horrors of American slavery, the abolitionists could now present a hunted black man in the English courts. This was a tremendous opportunity to reinvigorate the anti-slavery movement in England.

The application for habeas corpus ordering the sheriff of Toronto to 'bring up the body of John Anderson' was heard by the English Court of Queen's Bench on 15 January 1861. Presiding over the panel, and dominating his colleagues, was the chief justice, Sir Alexander Cockburn. After a brilliant career in the courts and Parliament, Cockburn had been appointed chief justice in 1856. Although he was considered the most distinguished jurist of the Victorian era, Cockburn retained a wistful attachment to the powers of government. It was rumoured that he had been reluctant to give up his cabinet position to become a judge, for 'Parliament [was] his element.'[14] Cockburn was also known to forgo a strict interpretation of the law to accommodate modern requirements. With this flexible and even political attitude to the law, Cockburn's court could be expected to take a different approach from Robinson's.

Despite the bitterly cold day the benches of the court at Westminster were filled with curious and sympathetic onlookers. The barristers' seats were crowded with learned gentlemen in horsehair wigs. Everyone waited upon the argument of the abolitionists' counsel, Edwin John James.[15] In his early years James had been an actor, but he had given up the profession when he was told that he looked too much like a prize-fighter. He had been a barrister since 1836, and he was noted for his success with juries, although (or perhaps because) 'he freely appealed ... to their ignorance and prejudices.' Never far from the public eye, James had recently been elected to Parliament. In the fall of 1860 he had visited Garibaldi's army before Capua. A flamboyant barrister such as James undoubtedly looked upon the Anderson case as an opportunity to gain publicity by representing a liberal cause while assisting an unfortunate fugitive.[15] 'With due and characteristic pomposity' James approached the judges' bench and began to plead the case. He began by reading the affidavit filed by Chamerovzow in support of the application. The affidavit stated that Anderson, 'a British subject,' was being illegally detained in Toronto. Unless a writ of habeas corpus was issued, he stood in grave and immediate danger.

None of the judges questioned the affidavit. How Louis Chamerovzow, who had never been to Canada and had never even laid eyes on John Anderson, could swear that he knew Anderson to be innocent of any crime was a mystery. Moreover, Anderson was not a British subject but an alien residing in British territory.[16]

Having introduced the affidavit without challenge, James continued. He maintained that the Crown still possessed the right to issue writs in Canada even though the colony had its own judicial system. Just because colonial courts existed did not mean that the authority of the queen had been ousted. English writs had been issued to Ireland, the Isle of Man, and other dependencies, and Canada stood in precisely the same position 'as a possession of the British Crown.'[17] James cited Vattel and Grotius as authority for the proposition that once a territory had been ceded or conquered, the laws of the conquering state extended to it. James quoted from Vattel's *Law of Nations*: 'Everything said of the territories of the nation must also extend to all the colonies.' Because the country had been conquered by the British Crown, he argued, British law applied to Canada. This was patently wrong. After the conquest of Quebec French civil law was allowed to prevail. Only when Upper Canada was separated from Lower Canada did the Upper Canadian legislature, in its first act, make the English law as it existed on 15 October 1792 the law of the province. After that date the provincial legislature would make its own laws. Moreover, Upper Canadian courts had ruled that some English laws were of no relevance or effect in the province.[18] None of this was brought to the court's attention, and the judges were left with the false impression that English law was to be automatically applied in Canada.

Much of James's argument was based on the issuance of a writ in 1389 to the English possession of Calais. The infamous Calais writ was part of an attempt by the House of Lords to rescue the Duke of Gloucester, the enemy of Richard II. Justice Blackburn intervened and advised James that Gloucester had been beheaded before the writ was executed. James replied that Gloucester had been smothered in a feather bed. 'Never mind how he died,' said an irate Blackburn. 'The writ of *habeas corpus* does not appear to have been effectual.' James conceded the point, but argued that another writ to Calais led to the trial of Gloucester's murderer.[19]

Justice Crompton broke into this erudite discussion and attempted to pin James down on the main issue. As Crompton saw it, the question was whether 'the courts in Westminster have now a concurrent jurisdiction with the local courts in granting this writ.' James argued that they did: 'The fact that Canada has both a separate legislature and judicature makes no difference. The Superior Courts in England have a concurrent jurisdiction with the courts in Canada as to issuing writs of *habeas corpus*.'[20]

Time and again James stressed that what was in question was the right of the Crown to issue the writ. 'It is the Queen's writ, it is her prerogative, as it has been called, to ascertain whether any of her subjects are rightly imprisoned.' Furthermore, this right was inherent in the Crown. This was too neat, too certain for the court, and the chief justice tried to articulate its difficulty in accepting James's argument: 'If the Crown does anything to take away from this court that jurisdiction [to issue *habeas corpus*] of course this court cannot exercise it.' The right to issue the writ did not vest in the person of Queen Victoria, but was governed by the local legislature. By creating local courts, had not the colony assumed the right to issue its own writs of habeas corpus? James persisted in citing cases in which English laws had been applied to colonies settled by Englishmen. Time and again the judges interrupted him to remind him that Canada had become a colony by conquest, not by settlement, and that those cases did not apply. James cited the case of *Ex Parte Lees*, where, he said, a writ of habeas corpus had issued to St Helena. Crompton J, who had heard the case, corrected him. The court had not issued the writ, and furthermore 'it is very doubtful whether we have the power [in those circumstances] to issue habeas corpus.' The mood of the court was definitely swinging against James.

Justice Crompton asked him bluntly if the Canadian courts had been created by the legislature or by the Crown. The case could hinge on this answer, for if the Canadian courts had been established by royal charter, then James's argument that habeas corpus was the 'queen's prerogative' was strengthened. If the courts had been created by the local legislature, that was all the more reason for the English courts to stay clear. James replied that the Canadian courts had been created 'by charter, under the Crown,' and he cited two statutes, 43 Geo. III, c.138 and the Quebec Act, 14 Geo. III, c.83. This greatly reassured the court, for a few moments later the chief justice declared that so long as the court was administering justice, 'on the part of the crown' the writ could be issued.[21]

Intentionally or not, Edwin James had seriously misled the judges. One act that he cited, 43 Geo. III, had merely extended the jurisdiction of existing Canadian courts and was of little or no relevance. The Quebec Act did indicate that courts were to be established under royal seal. However, far more relevant, and probably decisive, was the Canada Act of 1791. That statute had founded the province, and it stipulated that courts were to be established by the legislature, not by royal patent.[22] In 1794 this was accomplished, and the provincial legislature created its own Court of King's Bench.[23] The Upper Canadian courts were not extensions of the queen's prerogative; rather, they were creations of the colonial legislature. Had Chief Justice Cockburn known of the real state of the colonial courts, his views on the Anderson case might have been radically different. He was confused enough as it was, for at one point he had to ask James for the name of the Canadian court. It is difficult to understand how James, who had uncovered obscure medieval law, could have overlooked essential statutes. In any event, the court was left with the erroneous impression that Canadian courts were the creatures of royal prerogative. That meant that it was now likely to grant the writ.

As if the court were not already losing its way in a miasma of colonial law, James added to the confusion:

The Lord Chief Justice – When was the Court appointed? It must have been soon after the cession [of Canada to Britain in 1763].

Mr James – Yes, my lord, after the cession [actually, in 1794].

The Lord Chief Justice – And by the power of the Crown, by charter, not by the legislature.

Mr. James – That statute [14 George III, c.83] that I handed up to Mr Justice Hill is it [actually, by a colonial Act, 34 Geo. III, c.2, enacted twenty years later].[24]

James had effectively left a false impression that the writ of habeas corpus, the queen's prerogative, ran to the colonies until expressly revoked by the Crown. Chief Justice Cockburn still seemed uneasy with this unprecedented use of the court's power. Cockburn presumed that the Crown, by establishing local courts, had taken away this power of the English judiciary. A power affecting the liberty of the subject could never be taken away by a presumption, James argued. But, said the chief justice, did habeas corpus not derive from an English statute applying only to England? James replied that habeas corpus had its origins in the common law, which applied just as much to Canada as it did to England. Even so, the chief justice persisted, how could this court, thousands of miles removed from Canada, ensure that the writ was enforced? James, capable of meeting all challenges, replied, 'It cannot be assumed that the Queen's writ will not be obeyed.' The Toronto law officers were also British subjects, and it must be assumed that they would uphold the law.[25]

After a brief adjournment the judges returned, and the Chief Justice read their decision: the writ would issue, and John Anderson would be delivered up to the Westminster courts, which would decide whether he should be released. The chief justice expressed concern that the court's judgment 'may be said to be inconsistent with that high degree of colonial independence, both in legislation and judicature, which has carried into effect in modern times.' At the same time, he agreed with James that the court retained the right to issue habeas corpus to any British possession until that right was expressly taken away by Parliament.[26]

The court's decision was cheered by the spectators, although the demonstration was mild in comparison with that which had rocked Osgoode Hall.[27] The press was enthusiastic about the prospect of Anderson's appearing in an English courtroom. Once the case was safely in the hands of English judges, they thought, the fugitive would be safe. According to the *London Morning Star*, the hunted slave had appealed to the British lion for help, and not in vain. There was no fear, said the *Liverpool Mercury*, of English judges' 'torturing the plain and simple language' of the treaty. A case of this magnitude should be decided by imperial judges without reference to 'the by-laws of a little community.' The pleasure expressed by the English press at the issuance of the writ was mixed with a sneering condescension to the colonists. It was obvious, wrote the *London Standard*, that English courts 'have just as much right and control over all the British population of Canada as they have over her Majesty's subjects in Middlesex or Yorkshire.' And it was as well that this control existed as 'a salutary check to the frequent tyranny of the local courts of our colonies and dependencies.'[28]

For its part, the *Times* of London was delighted that the case was on its way to England, but expressed some uneasiness that Queen's Bench had issued a writ to the sheriff of Toronto 'as if Toronto were situate on Windermere instead of Lake Ontario.' According to the *Times*, Canada possessed all the trappings of self-government, and it seemed incongruous that an English court could interfere directly in a Canadian matter. In one of the most thoughtful comments on the Anderson case to appear in the British press, the *Times* questioned whether the issue justified an interference in colonial affairs. 'But a direct interposition of an English Court in the administration of justice in the colonies is, in our time at least, a novelty, and a novelty to justify the introduction of which very grave reasons are required.' Even so, the *Times* was certain that once the matter was in the hands of English judges, 'the question will be looked at in a larger and more comprehensive spirit by the English than it has been by the Canadian tribunals.' The *Times* editorialists observed that North Americans were too influenced by the nearness of the slavery struggle to render an impartial verdict. Moreover, the case, which involved the interpretation of an imperial treaty, was 'less suited for the judicature of the dependency than for the decision of the highest Court of the mother State.'

It was on this aspect of treaty interpretation that a vital element of British policy hinged. On the one hand, if the Webster-Ashburton treaty required Britain to return Anderson, then it would be a severe humiliation, as the *Times* noted: 'We, at least, are not accustomed to act as bailiffs or as gaolers for the Slaveowners of the South.' On the other hand, to refuse to return the fugitive would surely poison Anglo-American relations. It would be a damning censure of American policy, and ultimately 'a censure not likely to be soon forgotten or forgiven.' While the *Times* agreed that it was appropriate for Britain to decide the issue (and humanity dictated that it decide in favour of the fugitive), the assumption of jurisdiction would insult the Canadians and the refusal to extradite would surely antagonize the Americans.[29]

These unfortunate consequences were lost on a public whose sympathies were wholly with the fugitive. Already the case had been a boon to the anti-slavery movement. Money was flooding into the coffers of the British and Foreign Anti-Slavery Society in the eager expectation that '[Anderson] will be brought here and tried, and triumphantly acquitted.'[30] The prospect of the hunted black man standing before the bar gave the British public a chance to take part in the great drama that was unfolding across the Atlantic.

Although the popular press gave only superficial thought to the case and revelled in rumbustious 'come if you dare' challenges to the Americans, the legal journals considered seriously the issues that underlay the Anderson case. An editorial in the *Law Times* supported the conclusion of the Canadian judges. Chief Justice Robinson had not passed judgment for or against slavery, but had upheld the principle that to kill the person who held another in lawful custody was murder, and therefore extraditable: 'The conclusion of the [Canadian] Queen's Bench is strictly in accordance with the law, and it is right that it should be so, for it would be seriously mischievous to both the border countries, if criminals could obtain impunity by flying from one to the other.'[31] If the Webster-Ashburton treaty exempted fugitive slaves, as the newspapers and the abolitionists so vociferously maintained, then why was the treaty silent on any exemption? The *Law Times* was unique in recognizing the hypocrisy that pervaded the English denunciation of the Canadian judges. England had abolished slavery less than thirty years ago, and until then it had reaped immense profits from the institution. Indeed, it was England that had implanted slavery in the southern states.

The *Law Times* also exploded the myth of the assurances given to the English abolitionists that no slave would be extradited under Article x. George Denman, a prominent abolitionist and the son of a judge, had published a letter in the *Times* in which he repeated the assurances given by the government of the day that no fugitive slave was likely to be surrendered under the treaty.[32] The *Law Times* pointed out that reassurances given by politicians are not the law. Once a case was before the courts, the kind words of statesmen were no more relevant 'than a consultation between a solicitor and his client.'[33] It was the wording of the statute that must guide the judges. In addition, the ill-conceived writ now provided a method for an unscrupulous English lawyer to seek an ex parte application to snatch a criminal away from a colonial court in which he had been properly arraigned. The *Law Times* roundly condemned the issuance of the writ not only as bad law but as bad policy. The colonies were bound to see this act as an overthrow of their judicial independence and the subjugation of their courts to those of the mother country.

George Denman had arranged for the influential Juridical Society to hold a learned debate on the *Anderson* case. The general opinion was that natural-law principles applied to the case, and that all men had an intrinsic right to be free and to strike down a would-be enslaver. These views bore an uncanny resemblance to Freeman's unsuccessful plea before Queen's Bench. One young barrister, James Fitzjames Stephen, dismissed the talk of natural law as 'nothing more than a collective name for a number of theories of various writers.' Stephen thought that the Canadian judges were correct and that the crime must be established by examining the law of the place where it was committed. In later years Stephen was to become an outstanding criminal lawyer and eventually a judge of Queen's Bench.[34]

Once the Queen's Bench writ had been issued to Canada, the *Law Magazine* published an article by a barrister, Thomas Tapping, which thoroughly demolished the legal basis for the writ. The root of authority cited by James was the Calais writ, one of the most 'unconstitutional, atrocious and murderous transactions' in English history; it was a precedent for nothing.[35] Tapping faulted James for citing cases that did not concern habeas corpus or did not stand for the principles he said they did. With no one to argue against him, James had misled the court. Even more repugnant was James's refusal to look at the relevant legislation. He had presented a multitude of arguments with no proper foundation in the statute. The Canadian Fugitive Offenders' Act and the English Habeas Corpus Act should have been the first sources to be considered, not a dubious case from the reign of Richard II. Tapping maintained that the court should have been guided by the Habeas Corpus Act, which specified that the writ could issue only to England and its adjacent territories.[36] In recent cases the English courts had refused to issue writs to colonies. The previous chief justice, Lord Campbell, had doubted whether any English jurisdiction existed in a colony, and in *Doulson* v. *Mathews* the court had held that Westminster had no authority over acts that were 'in their nature local.'[37] In issuing the writ, Tapping said, Queen's Bench had overstepped its authority and set a dangerous and alarming precedent.

Legal opinions were by no means unanimous. The editor of the *Jurist* referred to Grotius for the proposition that a treaty could not be applied to a purely local crime, such as offences committed by slaves in Missouri. Extradition could only encompass acts that were, by common accord, serious crimes in *both* countries. Moreover, according to the natural law, any crime required malice aforethought. This element was missing in Anderson's case, for his only desire was to be free, not to kill Digges. The *Jurist*'s opinion was swayed by its strong anti-slavery leanings, for it declared that Britain never contemplated becoming the 'slave-driver' to America.[38] Likewise, the Scottish *Journal of Jurisprudence* doubted the correctness of the Canadian judges, and considered the issuance of the writ of habeas corpus from Westminster entirely appropriate. The Canadians had allowed local prejudices to blind them and had made a decision 'contrary to our natural policy.'[39] Those who supported Anderson derived solace from the natural law, from timeless principles that condoned any act performed to secure freedom. The jurists who thought the Canadian judges were correct tended to look at the wording of the treaty and the statutes, and based their opinion on the existing acts of Parliament.

Less than six months after the *Anderson* case, Queen's Bench had the chance to review this issue, and the judges seemed to agree with their critics that they had erred. In *Re Mansergh* (decided in June 1861) the same court of Queen's Bench considered the appeal of an officer to review an Indian court-martial. This time the court denied that it had any jurisdiction. Crompton J stated that a writ had issued in *Anderson* only because of the 'immediate danger' to the applicant. The *Anderson* case 'must not be taken as an authority that a habeas corpus will go to a colony.' Blackburn J had the same opinion: 'There is no authority that [Queen's Bench] will send a prohibition or a certiorari to the colonies.' He specifically repudiated the notion that 'we have a control over all jurisdictions beyond seas in countries subject to the British Crown.'[40] The *Anderson* decision had been based on a misleading argument and hastily formulated in concern for one individual's life. When the judges had the chance to reflect on the issue, they rejected the argument that there was a legal basis for issuing writs to colonies. It is illustrative of the precedent-bound and essentially illogical nature of the common law that by the twentieth century the decision in the *Anderson* case had become a binding rule. In 1910 the English Court of Appeal accepted without pause the principle in *Anderson*. According to one of England's most respected jurists, Vaughan Williams LJ, *Anderson* was the basis for the indisputable proposition that at common law English writs could issue to the colonies.[41] In 1957 the Court of Appeal issued a writ of habeas corpus to Northern Rhodesia. Lord Evershed MR said that 'the judgment in *Ex Parte Anderson* is, to my mind, historically at any rate, of considerable importance.'[42] With the dissolution of the British empire this question has become largely moot. However, it had another and possibly final reverberation in 1971, when the *Anderson* case was invoked by two detainees in Northern Ireland. The attempt failed, and the Court of Appeal held that a writ could not issue. Stephenson LJ cast some doubts on Edwin James's arguments in *Anderson*, and he referred to James as a counsel 'whose knowledge of the law has been said to be limited.'[43] More than a century after the events, James's reputation remained unsavoury. Nevertheless, he had persuaded Queen's Bench to adopt a rule which, though bad law and bad policy, became a precedent in English law.

The press anticipated that the Queen's Bench decision would be received by the Canadians with something less than rapture. The *Liverpool Post* warned that 'a dispute between this country and Canada seems inevitable.' Chief Justice Cockburn had expressed his misgivings at sending a writ to the colonies; the *Post* warned that 'the pride of the colony ... may be aroused, and the Canadians may refuse to permit an encroachment on their constitutional independence.'[44] Ever since the Durham Report of

1839 Britain had acquiesced in the granting of greater colonial autonomy. This attitude had enabled the emerging nations of Australia, Canada, and New Zealand to control their own internal affairs. Happily, it had also reduced the burden imposed on the British taxpayer to support the empire. Canada, for example, had arranged a reciprocity treaty with the United States in 1854 and had imposed a duty on British imports in 1859. Even the most paternal of imperialists 'viewed settlement colonies as developing nations which, according to an evolutionary process of historical growth, would mature and become self-governing at some point.'[45] The decision of Queen's Bench was a setback to this movement of nation-building and a denial that the settlement colonies had the right to conduct their own affairs. It usurped the authority of the local courts and implied the right of British authority to interfere at will. One writer predicted that Australia, 'already much inclined to claim independence,' would not bow to this kind of decision. It was sadly ironic, noted the writer, that 'the contest, begun by a runaway slave in Missouri, may result in depriving us of our greatest colonies.'[46]

Although the Duke of Newcastle had prohibited any attempt to return Anderson to Missouri, the government seemed content to wait and see what transpired in the courts. Both Newcastle and the Canadian governor, Sir Edmund Head, were believers in colonial autonomy, and they hesitated to interfere in a strictly local affair. Commenting on colonial tariff policies, the governor general had once said, 'However unsound the views of a community may be in matters of political economy, if that community substantially governs itself, we must expect to find such unsoundness reflected in its legislation. Self Government, which is only to operate when its acts agree with the opinions of others, is a contradiction in terms.'[47] In 1843 the imperial Parliament had devolved upon Canadians the power to deal with extradition. Now the colonial secretary purported to dictate to the Canadians the way in which those powers were to be exercised. The British government was committing the contradiction that Head had warned against. It had granted an authority which it was now trying to revoke. Only a few weeks before the Anderson case became a cause célèbre, a British magazine had boasted that 'Canada has acquired the conviction, that England has at length learned how to deal justly with her colonies.'[48] Some colonists now questioned the accuracy of that comment.

By early February 1861 the Anderson controversy had moved off the editorial pages and on to the floor of the House of Commons. On 8 February Henry Brinsley Sheridan asked the government whether

Cockburn's writ would arrive in Canada in time to save Anderson. If fugitive slaves were no longer safe in Canada, was it necessary to revise or even revoke the Webster-Ashburton treaty? Another member reminded the House that the Americans had recently refused to extradite Irish incendiaries under the pretence that they had committed political offences. The Anderson case proved the 'absurdity of the Ashburton treaty' and showed that it stood 'unrivalled as an instance of diplomatic incapacity and want of common sense.'[49] The normalization of relations between the United States and Britain which had been painfully put together in the early 1840s now seemed, as a result of the Anderson case, to be on the verge of unravelling.

The prime minister, Lord Palmerston, defended the treaty and assured the members that the government had issued strict instructions to the Canadians not to surrender the fugitive. 'Old Pam' probably sympathized with Anderson's cause. In July 1844 Palmerston had given the greatest speech of his life; he had argued eloquently for the suppression of the slave trade. While he was foreign secretary he had consistently defended the integrity of British territory as an asylum for fugitive slaves. Now he told the House that it was most unlikely that Anderson would be surrendered. Significantly, he noted that the question was ultimately to be decided by the governor general of Canada, and that the governor general was not to surrender the fugitive 'until the question shall have been fully considered by the Government at home, and until instructions shall be sent to him from hence.'[50] The governor general of Canada was to be responsible to the British, not the Canadian, cabinet.

This was an opinion calculated to outrage the Canadians. Colonial concern over British high-handedness was articulated by a Nova Scotia-born member of Parliament, Thomas Chandler Haliburton. On 22 February he rose in the House and inquired why a man with an 'unpronounceable name' had been permitted to seek a writ of habeas corpus in Canada. According to Haliburton, colonial rights had been violated in two respects: an English court had improperly sent a writ to Canada, and the British government had interfered in a purely local matter. By sending this order to the governor general of Canada the colonial secretary had deliberately violated the rights of the colonists. 'The Government of a constitutional colony was to be carried on by the Governor by and with the advice of his Council.' If Sir Edmund Head should obey this imperial decree, responsible government would be effectively subverted. 'If, therefore, any order went out which directed him to pursue a certain course without the advice of his Council, it would be a contravention of the constitutional rights of the people.' Haliburton had pointed out what everyone in the government from Lord Palmerston to the most junior minister seemed to have forgotten. Responsible government meant that the governor general was responsible to his colonial ministers, not to London. The Anderson controversy was a supreme example of imperial blundering. 'The Colonial Office seldom interfered in the colony at the right time,' raged Haliburton, 'and when it did interfere it usually did so in a wrong manner.'[51]

It was left to the dapper undersecretary for the colonies, Samuel Chichester-Fortescue, to blunt the effects of Haliburton's charges. He began in a disarming manner by complimenting the Canadian judges. Chief Justice Robinson had correctly found at the end of his judgment that the power to surrender the fugitive remained with the governor general. He minimized any talk of 'invasions' of the rights of the people of Canada. 'Just consider the nature of the case,' he argued. 'The controversy arises entirely out of a treaty concluded, not between the colony of Canada, but between the Imperial Government and the United States.'[52] It was obvious that on a question of international concern the British government could overrule the colonials. Left unsaid (or unconsidered) by Chichester-Fortescue was the fact that the question revolved around the interpretation of a provincial act, not the imperial treaty. Nevertheless, the government was satisfied that Haliburton had been answered satisfactorily. Outside the House, Chichester-Fortescue was complimented by Lord Palmerston and other senior members. The undersecretary recorded in his diary, 'In House, answered Haliburton, Sam Slick about Canadian Fugitive Slave Case. He was almost rebellious in his language, so loyal as to be nearly a rebel, like a true Orangeman.'[53]

But colonial outrage over the interference of the British courts and government in the Anderson affair could not be dismissed with a few reassurances. Chief Justice Cockburn's writ was on its way to Canada, and an explosion could be expected. The tumult over colonial rights was about to overshadow the prisoner sitting in the Brantford jail.

8

A Case of Quibbles

The American ambassador in London, George M. Dallas, was fully aware of the importance the administration attached to the Anderson case. He saw that court reporters were hired to take a record of the proceedings, and that a copy, still in shorthand form, was forwarded to Washington. Dallas reported that English sympathies had been aroused by the case and that all legal means would be exerted on the fugitive's behalf: 'It is scarcely necessary for me to remark on the pungent and uncompromising hostility to social bondage which prevails throughout this country.'[1] The report was directed to an administration that no longer held any real power. Even Buchanan's cabinet was badly divided between north and south. Secretary of State Lewis Cass had resigned in December over Buchanan's refusal to send troops to reinforce Charleston Harbour. His replacement, Jeremiah Black, had little time or desire to influence Anglo-American relations.

The north hoped for leadership from the president elect, Abraham Lincoln. His secretary of state designate, William Seward, still retained fanciful ideas that a war with Spain, France, or England (anyone would do) could serve to reunite the country. Even after session had begun, he maintained that in the event of an attack by a foreign power on New York 'all the hills of South Carolina would pour forth their population for the rescue.'[2] Of all potential enemies, the easiest to quarrel with would have been Britain.

News of the habeas corpus writ reached New York on 29 January 1861, and an anti-English reaction was immediately evident in the press. The *Baltimore American* noted that it was only because of the domestic crisis that Americans did not consider the grave consequences of this case.[3] The influential Democratic newspaper, the *New York Herald*, did consider the consequences, and was outraged by the English decision. 'Such is British observance of treaties,' fumed the *Herald*'s editor. 'This is but the beginning of our troubles with the English government. It can now afford to despise us.' The *Herald* linked the *Anderson* case with other grievances against Britain, and warned that if the British authorities refused to surrender Anderson 'they may expect retaliation in this country.'[4]

In the days following the *Anderson* decision the *Herald* published numerous articles on the 'impending revolution in the Canadas.' In the imagination of the *Herald*'s editors, the Canadians were so indignant at the English decision that they were preparing 'the declaration of their independence and the annexation of their territory.' Canada would trample this 'insulting despotism' underfoot by 'throwing off all that remains of the British yoke' and 'annex [ing] herself to the Northern confederacy without delay.'[5] In the day-dreams of the *Herald*, the northern states would receive Canada as consolation for the loss of the cotton states.

Perhaps even more fantastic was a Buffalo newspaper's assertion that the refusal to return Anderson was the root cause of southern disaffection. By assisting the abolitionist fanatics of the north, the Canadians were breaking the treaty and 'driving [the slave states] in self-defence to form a Southern confederation.'[6] According to this weird logic, the Canadians by their reluctance to give up Anderson had spawned the Confederacy!

Closer to reality was Thomas Henning, who feared that the British, in their eagerness to appease the Americans, would willingly give up the fugitive and make Canada 'a hunting ground equally with the Northern States.'[7] One Tennessee newspaper also expected this to happen, and rejoiced that the Canadian Queen's Bench decision had virtually broken up the underground railroad.[8] Yet many Americans, unable to help the escaped slaves in their own country, were determined to do all they could to preserve Canada as a haven. Gerrit Smith of New York had previously been to Toronto to help Anderson, and he again offered his services to the Anti-Slavery Society of Canada. A militant abolitionist, Smith had broken with the major political parties and churches over their compromise with slavery. For Gerrit Smith there was no compromise, and in the 1840s he became one of the founders of the 'Liberty Party,' the political wing of the abolitionists. He grew increasingly militant during the 1850s, and gave moral and financial support to John Brown's raid on Harpers Ferry, Virginia. When Smith proposed coming to Toronto to speak on the Anderson case, John Scoble gently tried to dissuade him. Smith's radicalism and his support for the failed raid on Harpers Ferry could have been embarrassing for the Canadians. Scoble did urge Smith to gather petitions from American abolitionists on this great issue, for 'we do not want to make it a question of color but of righteousness and holy law.'[9]

Nevertheless, Gerrit Smith was determined to come to Toronto, and on 15 January 1861 he spoke in St Lawrence Hall to the customary crowd of clergymen, sympathetic abolitionists, and local blacks. He began by saying that it would be difficult for him to give this speech in his own country. So strong was the mood of appeasement there that abolitionist gatherings were frequently broken up. Moreover, because of Buchanan's servility, the federal government had become an active agent of the slave-catchers. It was for these reasons that Canada had become the last hope of the American anti-slavery movement. Was it really possible, Smith asked, that in these dark hours Canada would recognize and apply the slave laws? How could the chief justice naïvely decide to return Anderson for 'trial' in Missouri? 'Does not your Chief Justice know that Anderson will scarcely have set foot within Missouri ere he will be seized by a mob, and amidst fiendish exultations be burnt at the stake?'[10] With no comprehension of the legal complexities of the case, Smith argued at length that it was never intended to make fugitive slaves subject to the Webster-Ashburton treaty. Like the English abolitionists, he had reached this conclusion after a private conversation with Lord Ashburton. Smith and another abolitionist leader, Lewis Tappan, had called on Ashburton before his departure from New York in 1842. The peer had assured them that the acts of slaves committed during an escape would not be considered extraditable. Yet, like all the others who had pronounced on these guarantees, Smith could not point to a clause in the treaty that exempted the fugitives.

Finally, he begged his listeners to keep up their pressure on the courts, for 'they are the most truly learned judges, who keep their ears open to the common sense of the common people.' To Gerrit Smith, the best judges heeded the voice of the people, not some words in dusty statute-books. The crisis over slavery in North America was reaching its climax, and the Anderson case was a crucial battle in the struggle. As Smith told his listeners, 'The influence of Great Britain in behalf of that cause has hitherto been great. Let it not be turned against it now ... We are now in our last struggle with the slave power. A very few years more, and that power will probably be either supreme over every part of the nation, or expelled from every part of it. Help us now them. Help us heartily.'

Despite this emotional appeal, Smith's speech had little impact on the case or on Canadian opinion. However, it was circulated throughout the free states, and generated a substantial awareness of the case and sympathy for Anderson. At the time Smith's speech was making the rounds, news of the English writ reached the United States. American abolitionists rejoiced at this turn of events. The editor of the Erie, Pennsylvania, *True American* congratulated Smith on his speech and lamented that while the Canadians were eager to help the fugitive slave, Washington was interested only in making further concessions to slaveowners. Another friend of Smith's, J.B. Sanborn, thought that the Anderson case would have an impact on the northern states' repeal of the Personal Liberties Acts. These statutes, which had been passed to frustrate the effect of the Fugitive Slave Act of 1850, were being repealed in an effort to appease the south. How could the north repeal them when England had set the morally correct example by refusing to give up Anderson?

Angelina Grimké Weld, the 'angel of light' of the anti-slavery movement and one of the first women to lecture on the evils of slavery wrote to Smith: 'What a triumph for the cause of Humanity – that Great Britain should think the "poor nigger" so despised & trodden down, of so much consequence as to have him brought all the way to England to ensure his liberty.' And what a blow to 'slavocracy': 'How the South must gnash her teeth with rage & utterly despair of the sympathy & help which She flattered herself. King Cotton would certainly force England to give the new Confederacy.'[11]

Mrs. Weld had touched a sore spot. The Anderson case should have shown southerners of how their new nation was perceived. To southerners the British reaction to the Anderson case should have been an indication of their chances of getting diplomatic recognition. The outpouring of anti-slavery sentiment proved that slavery was still a potent political factor in Britain. As Ambassador Dallas had observed, the Anderson case had aroused the English hatred of, as he delicately called it, 'social bondage.' As it was, southerners persisted in the delusion that because the British textile industry relied on southern cotton Britain would swallow its qualms and recognize the Confederacy.[12]

A Charleston, South Carolina, newspaper quoted the *Toronto Leader* to the effect that Great Britain would soon recognize the Confederacy.

Southern newspapers interpreted the decision of Robinson's court as ordering the return of Anderson to Missouri, and they concluded from this that British America would now co-operate in the return of other escaped slaves. Even the pro-southern *New York Herald* thought that the Anderson case proved 'that the Canadians themselves are not so extreme in their anti-slavery feelings.'[13] The initial Canadian decision on the Anderson case led many southerners to believe that there would be business as usual between the Confederacy and Britain.

Southerners should have heeded the *New York Times*'s comment that, to the contrary, the Anderson case had shown the extent of the British antipathy to the slave states, that 'the [Anderson controversy] foreshadows, at the very dawn of a new Southern Empire, the grave difficulties that must continually arise between a Slave Confederacy and the great Anti-Slavery Power of the world.' The new government in Montgomery, Alabama, ought to have recognized the accuracy of the *Times*'s observation: 'In this determination of Great Britain to protect the fugitive, and in the overwhelming popular sympathy that the fate of Anderson has excited, our Southern politicians may learn the monstrous absurdity of their hope that a Confederacy based upon Slavery will ever be recognized by the Government or people of England.'[14]

The Anderson case had shown to many thoughtful Americans that British recognition of a republic based on slavery would be slow to come. Yet as the secession crisis worsened, Americans turned all their attention to the looming civil war. Secretary of State Black all but ignored foreign affairs, and while Senator James Green of Missouri raised the *Anderson* case in the Senate, his only comment was a request for information.[15] Americans lost interest in the *Anderson* case and in Britain's obvious reluctance to enforce the extradition treaty.

Canadians, however, drew a far more enduring lesson from the English writ of habeas corpus. An English court was now preparing to override local courts on a matter of local concern. Men had died during the Rebellion of 1837, a rebellion that had led to the granting of self-governing institutions and a government responsible to the people. Responsible government enabled Canadians to direct their own internal affairs, and that prerogative was hard-won and jealously guarded. The decision of Chief Justice Cockburn was a direct negation of the right of Canadians to control one of their most important institutions, the courts. On this one issue (and it was remarkable that they could come together on any issue) both conservatives and reformers were united in outrage.

When news of the English writ first reached Montreal, the reaction was one of incredulity. Surely there had to be some error in the transmission, for no English court could presume to issue a writ in Canada. The Montreal reaction to the news reflected popular feelings. The common people openly rejoiced, and there were calls for bonfires of celebration. Editorialists were shocked by this invasion of Canadian sovereignty, however. The *Montreal Gazette* a caustic critic of Macdonald and a valuable supporter of Anderson, wrote that the English writ was 'a forgery or mere literary curiosity ... it is a dangerous infringement of our franchises.'[16]

'So arrogant a claim' was the way in which the *Globe* characterized Cockburn's decision. The infringement on the rights of the Canadian judiciary had caused 'an unwonted excitement' within the stately walls of Osgoode Hall. The lawyers and indeed the entire community were outraged at the 'attempted violation of those principles of self-government which it was thought had been firmly established in Canada.'[17] The *Globe* demanded that the English court be directed to 'mind its own affairs' in England and abstain from interference in other countries. Another opposition newspaper, the *Brantford Expositor* considered these '*dictums* of Westminster Hall' to be an 'insult to the People of Canada and their law courts.'[18]

To the ministerial press, the English decision was 'an apparent interference with the rights of this country.'[19] According to the government's supporters in Montreal, the English court 'has no more right to take cognizance of this case than our Courts would have to interfere with a matter before an English tribunal.'[20] Probably the most vociferous denunciation of the decision came from the *Toronto Leader*. In almost revolutionary language, it declared:

Probably no similar attempt has been made within our day to encroach on the liberties of a free people. Canada, a great self-governing community, with a commercial tonnage more than twice that of France, is compared to the Isle of Jersey and the Isle of Man ... If the judicial branch of our government may be trenched upon, in this summary manner, who is to guarantee the executive and legislative functions of government from invasion?[21]

Outrage at the case was not limited to politicians and pressmen. At a grand dinner held in honour of a liberal politician, Adam Wilson, the matter of the English action was raised. 'If I gather rightly the opinions of the electors of the North Riding of York,' said Wilson, 'they would totally and decidedly condemn its unconstitutionality and deny its expediency.'

Even at the community level, resentment of the English decision was beginning to overshadow sympathy for Anderson. Wilson, a respected lawyer, admitted that English courts had the right to issue writs in Canada. Nevertheless, it was unwise to exercise such a discretion, for the situation 'is the making of a very pretty quarrel.'[22]

The Canadian legal establishment made its response in the pages of the *Upper Canada Law Journal*.[23] The decision of Cockburn's court was contrary to the English Habeas Corpus Act and was not based on any reliable precedent. James had cited *Ex Parte Lees* as proof that English writs ran to the island of St Helena. But the case, read correctly, stood for just the opposite conclusion: the court had refused to issue a writ to St Helena. Moreover, the basis for the writ, Chamerovzow's affidavit, was a gross distortion of the facts. Anderson was not a British subject, and it was not clear that he was innocent of all wrongdoing. The decision was not only bad law, it was 'dangerous to our colonial independence.' Even though Canadians were 'pushing forward to take our place on the pedestal of nations, we have well nigh forgotten the acts of colonial misrule under which we at one time suffered.' The *Anderson* case was a reminder of colonial misrule, and the *Journal* urged that it be speedily reversed by Parliament. Strangely, the report in the *Journal* contained no reference to Edwin James's having misled Queen's Bench on the origins of the Canadian courts. This is probably because the only available record of the case appeared in the English *Law Times*, and that version had omitted the discussion of the issue.[24] Had they known all the facts, the Canadian lawyers' outrage might have been redirected towards James and the English abolitionists.

The *Anderson* case had become a tug-of-war between an emerging colony and an intransigent empire. In all this controversy everyone seemed to have forgotten about the prisoner. John Anderson remained locked up in Brantford at the not-too-tender mercies of William Mathews. A letter to the *Globe* signed by 'Africanus' (who called herself 'a wife and mother, and one of the down-trodden race to which she [Anderson's wife] belonged') asked what the fugitive's supporters were doing to help his wife and family, who were in need of money as well as sympathy.[25] This is the only mention of John Anderson's family in Canada. His memoirs, compiled later, make no reference to a Canadian family; if he had any such family he abandoned them when he left Canada.

Even before Robinson's court had ruled against him, Samuel Freeman had been considering various avenues of appeal. Oliver Mowat had also appeared on behalf of the prisoner and had inquired whether the attorney general would consent to an appeal before the Court of Error and Appeal.[26] Freeman asked for the government's help, and reminded the attorney general that if he was successful he would relieve the minister of a very embarrassing obligation.[27] John A. Macdonald needed no reminding. He assured Freeman that the government would consent to any appeals he might wish to bring. Freeman thanked the attorney general, and indicated that he would take the appeal to the province's highest court, the Court of Error and Appeal, in February. If he was unsuccessful there, he would try for another writ of habeas corpus in the Court of Common Pleas.[28]

Upon receiving news of the English writ, Freeman changed all these plans. Speed was now essential, for a special courier had delivered the writ to Thomas Henning of the Anti-Slavery Society. The struggle for the body of John Anderson had reached a critical stage, with both Canadian and English courts vying for the case. On 1 February 1861 Freeman asked Chief Justice Draper of the Court of Common Pleas for a writ of habeas corpus. Draper reminded Freeman that Chief Justice Cockburn had ordered Anderson to appear before him in London. 'Yes, my lord, it so appears,' replied Freeman, 'but I am desirous of obtaining the opinion of the Common Pleas in this Province.' Draper looked down from the bench: 'Mr Freeman, take the writ,' was his response.[29]

Samuel Freeman wrote to Macdonald that he had no doubt of success. In the next line, however, he tempered his enthusiasm by commenting that if he were unsuccessful he would appeal still further. Freeman was as eager as Macdonald for Anderson to be liberated by a Canadian court, and he hoped that Common Pleas would settle the matter 'without the interference of the Courts in England unsolicited.'[30] The case was scheduled to be heard in a week's time, on Friday, 8 February. There was little doubt that this was the final opportunity to resolve this momentous question in the province.

This time Sheriff Jarvis was taking no chances; he ordered that all persons who wished to attend should first apply to his office for a ticket. Osgoode Hall had sustained considerable damage from the near riot during the last hearing, and the sheriff was not about to tolerate a repetition. Strangely, however, the public was not nearly as aroused in February as it had been in December. The hearing was delayed till 9 February, and on that day there was a much smaller and more orderly crowd present in the courtroom. No troops or armed police were required for the occasion, and there seemed to be a general feeling that 'in some way or other Anderson will be saved from being sent back to Missouri.'[31]

It was in this sedate atmosphere that the judges of Common Pleas prepared to hear the argument.

Common Pleas made a curious contrast with its senior court, Queen's Bench. Robinson and McLean of Queen's Bench had been appointed in 1829 and 1837 respectively, and to much of the province they represented the genteel autocracy of earlier days. The judges of Common Pleas had been appointed during the age of responsible government, and they could be expected to take a far more progressive view of the law. Even though the chief justice of Common Pleas, William Henry Draper, was a former conservative leader, he was far more liberal in outlook than most of his tory brethren.[32] His two associate justices, John Hawkins Hagarty and William Buell Richards, had been pronounced liberals in their day. Richards had been an enthusiastic reformer and an early supporter of George Brown.[33] He had sat as a reformer in the legislature and served as attorney general until his appointment to the bench in 1853. John Hagarty was as much a reformer on the bench as he had been in law practice.[34] He used his judicial position to condemn the vices he thought were destroying society. In 1857 he had warned that 'an ulcer is eating into the vitals of our social system in the shape of crowds of people growing up in neglect and ignorance, rapidly ripening into crime, too many of them destined to form the chief population hereafter of our Gaols and Penitentiaries.'[35] Chief Justice Robinson, who did not share these gloomy views, had rebuked Hagarty: 'some of my brother judges in this place have, I perceive, felt themselves called on to remark on the increase of crime in the younger part of the population, and also the great extent to which the crime of drunkenness had increased ... [T]here is, I think, no country in the world in which one would expect to find less room for such remarks.'[36]

Assisting Freeman were two more barristers, Matthew Crooks Cameron and Thomas Hodgins. The court would listen to only two speakers, so Freeman and Cameron spoke for the prisoner. The addition of Cameron made the defence bipartisan, for he was a noted conservative. Indeed, he was widely known for his political self-reliance. Only a few days earlier he had lost the Toronto mayoralty contest, a defeat the *Globe* attributed to Cameron's having opposed the powerful Orange Lodges.

Freeman opened his argument in much the same way as he had before Queen's Bench.[37] He said that there was insufficient evidence of murder by Canadian standards, that the prisoner's acts had to be judged by Canadian law, and that in any event Missouri's slave laws were contrary to natural justice. By striking Seneca Digges Anderson had been defending his liberty, and the act could not constitute murder according to Canadian norms. Referring to the evidence, Freeman argued that the prisoner's only hope of escape lay in violence. In order to justify his argument Freeman had to paint a vivid picture of slavery for the court. Still arguing as if he were appealing to a jury, he cited illustrations of the barbarity of slavery. A white man who raped a female slave bore no criminal responsibility; at most, the slave's owner could bring a civil action for damage to goods.[38] Slaves who attempted to escape could have a cat dragged back and forth over their bare backs or be mutilated or branded for future identification. This was proof of the base system which Anderson was justified in resisting by force.

Not only was the prisoner justified in using force, Freeman said, he had not used excessive force. Chief Justice Robinson had concluded that Anderson had done far more violence than was necessary to resist capture. In Robinson's words, Anderson had *turned upon* [Digges] having an open knife in his hand, and ran at him.' Freeman argued that the depositions did not support such a conclusion. According to the Missouri witnesses, the incident was only the briefest collision; there had been no time for thought or malice. As Freeman described it, 'a moment of time elapsed between the striking of the two blows.'[39] When the facts were seen in this light, the most Anderson could be charged with was the non-extraditable offence of manslaughter. Chief Justice Draper doubted this. He commented, 'Homicide in all cases *prima facie* and unexplained is murder.'[40]

Freeman then raised a technical objection. There was no indication that Missouri had ever charged Anderson. A charge under Missouri law was a precondition to extradition proceedings. Draper interrupted and pointed out that according to the statute it was necessary only that a requisition be made by the proper state official. The question then arose whether the court could recognize Missouri state laws. Justice Hagarty asked whether the slave act was peculiar to Missouri or a general law of the United States. 'You are not to presume anything against the prisoner,' replied Freeman. Chief Justice Draper looked down angrily from the bench, and reminded Freeman that he was addressing one of Her Majesty's judges: 'We are talking of points of law, and your remark is not applicable.' Freeman had obviously made no headway with the technical objections, and he wistfully dropped the point.

Freeman returned to the one argument upon which his case ultimately rested. In extradition cases 'double criminality' must exist; that is, the act must be an offence against the law of the state in which extradition is sought as well as an offence in the state in which the act was committed. 'The acts of Digges in endeavouring to capture Anderson, as well as Anderson's resistance, are to be judged by our law.'[41] Under Canadian law Digges had no right to enslave Anderson, and it was his act, not Anderson's homicide, that was illegal. It was the very illegality of Digges's act that justified Anderson's act. British law could not recognize slavery in any form; as authority Freeman cited the *Creole* case of 1841 and Lord Denman's comment that 'no nation is entitled to enforce the law of another country which is founded in injustice.' Draper cut in again and asked if it were not true that some of the slaves in *Creole* were tried for murder. Freeman had no ready answer, so he leaned over the counsel table and discussed the point with John Scoble of the Anti-Slavery Society. He replied that they were not tried. 'Then,' continued Draper, 'the only official account that I have seen which professes to be authentic, is wrong.' The judges corrected Freeman and Scoble's version of the *Creole* case and pointed out that not only were some of the *Creole* mutineers tried, compensation was paid to the United States.[42] Obviously, Britain did give limited recognition to slave laws in its dealings with the United States. The keystone of Freeman's case had suddenly crumbled.

Concluding his argument much as he had begun it, Freeman made an impassioned appeal to the judges to apply the natural law. 'This Missouri law is against natural justice, and the authority of that state to make such a law will not be presumed.'[43] He ended with a typical flourish and asked the judges to bid Anderson 'go forth from this temple of justice' a free man. However, it must have been apparent to everyone in the courtroom that not one of the arguments raised by Freeman had found favour with the judges.

If Freeman had made no headway with the court, his associate, Matthew Cameron, was equally unsuccessful. The homicide was justifiable, said Cameron, because 'Anderson was in insurrection against an unnatural law.' He compared Anderson to the rebels who threatened any day to fire on Fort Sumter. If one of those rebels was apprehended in Canada, would he be extradited for having killed a federal soldier? Justice Hagarty wryly answered that whether they were murderers or patriots would depend upon their degree of success. A slave, Cameron maintained, 'had a right to rebel.'[44] The chief justice dismissed this argument and cited an English statute that recognized the legality of slavery.[45]

As the *Anderson* case showed, the argument of an appeal does not consist of a lawyer's reading a set speech. It is a process of give and take between lawyers and judges in which the issues are often turned around and looked at from new perspectives. A good appeal counsel must be prepared to examine hypothetical situations that he had never considered before entering the courtroom. In this way a legal issue almost takes on a life of its own as lawyers and judges continually refine the issue. Using hypothetical cases, Chief Justice Draper tried to get Cameron to admit that slaves are subject to the laws of their locality:

Chief Justice Draper – Mr Cameron, take the case of a white man killing a slave. Have you any doubt he would be given up?

Mr Cameron – We would give him up.

Chief Justice Draper – Then you say if the slave killed a white man he should not be given up.

Mr Cameron – No, I do not say when a slave kills a white man, when the killing is not necessary to secure his liberty, that he does not commit murder.

Chief Justice Draper – The moment you admit that, you admit his liability to the municipal laws of the country in which he lives.

Having established that at least to some degree slaves were liable to local laws, the chief justice pursued the matter further:

Chief Justice Draper – If a slave commits a murder –putting his state of slavery altogether out of the question –according to our law, if he escaped, would it be our duty to give him up?

Mr Cameron – I think so.

Chief Justice Draper – Then that takes away the notion of treating him as a chattel, and that he is not responsible for his acts. Follow that out. Is he liable to be given up then whether or not the act which he has done be justifiable becomes a question of law?

Mr Cameron – It is a question of law when the facts are found.

The chief justice's point was apparent. Slaves were responsible for their acts and had a duty to obey the municipal laws. Therefore, if slaves could commit murder, they could be extradited pursuant to the treaty. Because the statute gave the magistrate the power to determine on the facts what constituted murder, the judges were powerless to interfere. The case in favour of extradition now seemed impregnable.

In fairness to Cameron and his client, the chief justice continued to probe for arguments that might help the prisoner:

Chief Justice Draper – Then your argument resolves itself to this – that murder is murder *prima facie*, but it becomes justifiable homicide because the prisoner was asserting his freedom.

Mr Cameron – Yes, that is it.

Chief Justice Draper – You then say a slave may commit murder, but that in this case, circumstances may justify him?

Mr Cameron – I say so, because we must judge of this murder according to our notions of law and right, and that we cannot import anything from Missouri contrary to them.

The trouble with this reasoning was that it required the court to apply its 'notions of law and right' to negate the slave laws of Missouri. How could one country, which had entered into a treaty relationship with another, arbitrarily dictate that some of the other country's laws were repugnant and should not be recognized? The judges put the simple question to Cameron: leaving aside the question of slavery, was the killing of a guard by a prisoner murder? Cameron refused to concede this point, but maintained that slavery justified the homicide. Time and again the judges asked Cameron to omit slavery from the equation and answer the hypothetical question whether a prisoner who killed his jailer had committed murder:

Mr Justice Hagarty – Put the slave out of the question altogether. If our Police Magistrate sends a constable to arrest a man for the infraction of a city by-law, and the arrest is resisted, and the slayer flies to Missouri, I wish to know whether, unless the same by-law was the law of Missouri, could the fugitive be delivered up?

Mr Cameron – Yes. Because the person who has to be delivered up is one who has the same rights as other people.

Mr Justice Hagarty [in despair] – That's the slave again![46]

The bedrock of Cameron's argument was the sinister institution of slavery. Once again Anderson's lawyers had gambled his life on the proposition that because slavery was intrinsically evil, he had done nothing wrong in resisting it. This was stirring rhetoric but unconvincing law.

With his case practically won, Henry Eccles rose to present the case for the Crown. He was there to argue a point of law, not to speak for or against slavery. His colleagues Cameron and Freeman 'seemed to have imagined that they were standing on the floor of Parliament ... or that they were addressing some public meeting on the hardships of slavery.'[47]

The Crown wished only to argue the law; it would leave emotions to the editorial pages. Eccles was about to get more of an argument than he expected. The chief justice wanted to know why a political matter had been brought to court. Eccles replied rather lamely that it was Freeman who had first suggested this course to the government. Draper then asked a series of questions about the form and sufficiency of ther warrant of commitment. The chief justice had noticed that the warrant made no mention of the word 'murder': 'Chief Justice Draper said that if the prisoner had never been committed for murder – if he was not charged with murder – he did not see how it was possible the Court could declare him to be in legal custody. They had no right to commit him for any other offence ... how was he in custody at all?[48] The warrant did refer to Anderson's 'wilfully, maliciously and feloniously' stabbing and killing Seneca Digges. Nowhere was the all-important word 'murder' used. Eccles had no good answer to this challenge, and he turned the case over to Robert Harrison.

The judges permitted Harrison to rebut the defence's arguments on the merits of the case. In his usual comprehensive way, Harrison showed that extradition in these circumstances was necessary. Crime was inseparable from locality, and it was essential that the magistrate who was examining a request for extradition look at the laws of the place where the act was committed. To illustrate his point, Harrison cited an American case, In Re Fetter.[49] A California resident had committed statutory fraud and fled to New Jersey. He pleaded that New Jersey had no statutes of fraud similar to California's. Nevertheless, the court held that he had committed a criminal act in California and must be returned. For extradition purposes 'each power accepted the law of the other country without enquiry for the purposes of the treaty, or else the treaty is a dead letter.' A Canadian court had no right to pass judgment on Missouri laws, but must accept the fact that 'in each country, to kill when in legal custody is murder.' To deny this would be to 'put an end to the treaty from the first moment of its existence.'[50]

This was a powerful argument, and the court was not in a mood to challenge it. Instead, the judges queried Harrison about the defective warrant. Justice Hagarty pointed out that the statute required the magistrate to certify an offence. The warrant specified no offence at all, and it could be questioned whether the magistrate had reached any conclusion. Harrison suggested that the words 'feloniously and maliciously did kill' were the equivalent of 'murdered.' When pressed on the point, Harrison had to admit that the warrant was probably defective.[51]

The question then arose whether Anderson's committal by Queen's Bench had remedied the defect. Harrison doubted that the defect had been cured, and did not wish to press the point.

William Mathews's improperly worded warrant was the guarantee of John Anderson's freedom. The bumbling racist Mathews had, through his incompetence (he had made an almost identical error in an extradition warrant only nine months before the Anderson case),[52] proved himself the fugitive's best friend. When the court rose at twenty minutes after seven, there was little doubt of the result. After eight and a half hours of continuous argument the judges had decided to release the prisoner on a technicality. Chief Justice Draper announced the court's determination to make a decision soon so that Anderson could be released from custody.

'A quibble about the warrant' was the way the *Globe* viewed the proceedings. It was disgraceful that the great question should be decided by 'all the hair-splitting arguments of lawyers and all the bamboozling questions and puzzling cases of judges.'[53] The case was such a 'mass of legal and technical verbiage' that few observers could understand it.[54] The only thing that seemed clear was that John Anderson would soon be a free man again.

The abolitionists had an uncanny knack for creating ill will. Now that Anderson was in the Toronto jail, Henning served the English writ on Sheriff Fred Jarvis. Cockburn's court had addressed the writ to the sheriff of Toronto, and so long as Anderson remained in Brantford it was unenforceable. On 11 February, when Anderson was in the Toronto jail waiting for the decision of Common Pleas, Henning saw his chance to serve the proper officer. Coolly, Jarvis told Henning that although he respected the English judges, he had had no formal instructions in the matter and would wait upon direction from the Canadian courts. [55] Failure to obey the writ could have left the sheriff open to a civil action. For the moment, however, he put the writ aside. Other Canadians urged him to ship the writ back to England 'like a dishonored bill of Exchange.'[56] For the moment, everything hinged on the decision of Common Pleas.

By Saturday, 16 February 1861, the judges of Common Pleas were ready to give their verdict. This time there was no doubt about the outcome. Because the courtroom was so crowded, Anderson was seated in the front semi-circle that was usually reserved for Queen's Counsel. Chief Justice Draper gave his decision first, and he all but ignored the defence's ringing phrases about the curse of slavery. His main interest was in the defective warrant. The warrant had used only the word 'kill,' and that could mean manslaughter or even justifiable homicide. Because it failed to specify 'murder' the warrant did not describe an extraditable offence. Another fatal objection to the warrant was its failure to specify that Anderson was being held until surrendered to Missouri or discharged according to law. In another glorious miscue, Bill Mathews had worded the warrant to say that the prisoner shall be imprisoned until delivered by due course of law. This was not the wording the Fugitive Offenders' Act required, and it was not apparent, in a remarkable aside, that the judges had agreed that this defect voided Anderson's imprisonment.

Draper revealed that only a few days before the last hearing he had discussed Anderson's case with Chief Justice Robinson.[57] Robinson had shown Draper a copy of an English case, *Ex parte Besset*,[58] which was exactly on point. In that case the magistrate had also committed the accused until discharged by due course of law. This did not conform to the statute, and the prisoner was released. This criminal case, the precedent that mandated Anderson's freedom, had been discovered by Robinson and brought to Draper's attention. The two chief Justices had, in their chambers, read the case and decided that Anderson should be released because of the faulty writ: ironically, the decision to liberate Anderson had been made before the eight-and-a-half-hour ordeal in Common Pleas.

At the end of his decision Draper said that except for the defects in the warrant he would have agreed with the decision of Queen's Bench. It was ludicrous, he thought, to declare that '4,000,000 of slaves in the southern states may commit assassination in aid of escape.'[59] Justice Richards agreed that the warrant was hopelessly defective. Because it failed to specify 'murder' it was doubtful whether the magistrate had concluded that there was enough evidence to support any charge. Having dismissed the case on this technicality, Richards would not deal with the merits. The last judge to speak, John Hagarty, agreed with his colleagues that the technical flaws in the warrant were so grave that it had to be quashed. He also dealt with the issues raised by Cameron and Freeman, particularly the argument that in weighing the prisoner's acts no account could be taken of Missouri law. Hagarty felt that such an interpretation 'might insure impunity to the mass of offenders, white and coloured.' Extradition was a useful tool of international justice, and it was essential that Canada give some recognition to the laws of foreign states: 'Lastly, that the contracting parties are to surrender or refuse to surrender, according to their view of the justice or the injustice, the equity or the iniquity of the law said to have been violated. This must lead to endless disputation, and leave the treaty either to utter disuse, or to a capricious and offensive execution.'[60]

Surprisingly, two of the judges, Draper and Hagarty, had sided with the majority of Queen's Bench by implying that Anderson should be extradited on the merits of the case. The two courts had both applied the same principles in their interpretation of the act. Instead of relying on 'natural law,' the judges had preferred the utilitarian principle that because extradition was necessary for international justice a recognition of the mutuality of state laws was beneficial. If the government entered into a treaty with a country that permitted slavery, then so be it. The judges must enforce the law.

The spectators in the courtroom were entirely unaware that any utilitarian principle was being applied. They did understand that the court was ruling in favour of the prisoner, and they punctuated each judge's verdict with cheers and foot-stamping. When Sheriff Jarvis told Anderson that he was now free to go, a ripple of applause went through the court. Anderson stood up uncertainly and said to the judges, 'Thank you, gentlemen – thank you, your lordships.' The crowd was pressing into the courtroom, and Anderson was led out through the judge's chambers to the main exit of Osgoode Hall. He was immediately acclaimed by the crowd, and one black spectator called for three cheers for the British government. Toronto lay under a covering of snow, and a sleigh was called for to take Anderson around the city in what was nothing less than a triumphal parade. For weeks the newspapers had celebrated this black Garibaldi, and the time had arrived for his public acclamation.[61]

Before the procession left Osgoode Hall, Anderson had to make one sudden and far-reaching decision. Waiting for him in the courtyard were his black friends and supporters, fellow fugitives who had almost stormed the Simcoe jail and who had ridden in his posse to Brantford. Also in attendance outside Osgoode Hall were the well-to-do abolitionists of Toronto, who, through the efforts of men such as John Scoble and Toronto alderman John Nasmith had rallied the newspapers and the people to Anderson's cause.

Scoble elbowed his way through the crowd and shouted for Anderson to join him. Surrounded by his black friends and neighbours, he seemed reluctant to leave their company. A white onlooker leaned over and said to him, 'Yes, go with Mr Scoble, Anderson, if it had not been for him you would not have got your liberty.' He considered this, and went over to his black friends to have a few words with them. Then he got in the sleigh and drove off with Scoble and Nasmith.[62] By leaving with those men he also left his old life. He could never return to the simple duties of a mason in

Caledonia. Not only had John Anderson become a public figure, he was still a wanted man. It was possible that an extradition warrant could be reissued (this time in proper form) and that he could be jailed pending his return to Missouri. His only hope lay with the support of white abolitionists, and he was henceforth under their protection and control.

'Thus has a very satisfactory conclusion been arrived at,' wrote the *Quebec Chronicle*, 'in a very unsatisfactory way.' Abolitionists were dismayed that 'no principle has been established, no right vindicated' by Anderson's release.[63] They had hoped for a glorious denunciation of slavery and instead had been given a disheartening lecture on proper form. Anderson was not the only one to be freed by the decision of Common Pleas. Attorney General Macdonald had escaped from the proceedings almost unscathed. The liberal press still grumbled about 'our slave-catching government';[64] the *Globe* was particularly incensed by the result: 'The appeal to legal technicalities was simply an evasion of [Macdonald's] duty – the case was not one to be determined by nice legal rules, but on broad grounds of national policy.'[65] Yet even the government shared in the public's feeling of relief that followed Anderson's release. After all, the government had ensured that he had received every legal advantage. 'Wonder what the *Globe* will now do for sensation articles?' wrote one of Macdonald's supporters. 'Anderson has proved a god-send to it for the last six months, and kept its scribblers from rusting.'[66] Even liberal observers were relieved to finally have the case over. 'We profess ourselves to be not at all squeamish. The great object sought, the delivery of Anderson from the hands of his pursuers, has been obtained.'[67] Across the province people rejoiced at Anderson's liberation and took little note of the way in which it had been accomplished.

There remained one last piece of business, the piece dearest to the heart of every lawyer who knows he has a client with unlimited funds. Two days after Anderson's release Freeman wrote to Macdonald to report on the case. He concluded: 'The next thing is my Bill of Costs. In what form shall I sent it?'[68]

9

'To Make a Demigod of Him'

The pro-government newspapers fervently hoped that Anderson's case would fade away. The *Hamilton Spectator* expected the fugitive to be 'transmogrified into a plain, common negro again,' and thought that he would become as insignificant 'as when he disturbed the hen-roosts up at Caledonia.' All things must come to an end, wrote the *Spectator*, 'and so has the world-wide Extradition case.'[1] But instead of fading away, John Anderson was just beginning to emerge as a living symbol of the struggle against slavery.

A few days later after his release he gave his first public speech at the Queen Street Baptist Church in Toronto. He told his listeners that while he was happy to greet them, he was unused to speaking in public. He urged his fellow blacks to unite in the struggle. He begged his white supporters not to make a hero of him, for he was well able to work and look after himself. It was at this meeting that he first told an audience that while in jail he had dreamed that an eagle would carry him off, but that the Lion of England had protected him. The crowd warmed to his humility and took patriotic pride in his simple metaphor.[2]

The chairman of the meeting the Rev. Dr Michael Willis, announced that the Anti-Slavery Society of Canada had not yet made 'arrangements' for Anderson. (Apparently it was not contemplated that he should make his own.) There was some hint that he might stay in Canada; the society had obtained a grant of 100 acres for the fugitive. There were also suggestions that he emigrate to the West Indies. However, his destiny was ultimately to be decided by a group of London ministers. The newly formed London Emancipation Society, fully aware of Anderson's symbolic value, invited him to come to England in March 1861. Samuel Freeman worried that Anderson could be re-arrested (this time according to the proper form) and again face the ordeal of extradition proceedings. He joined with John Scoble in urging that Anderson travel to England for his own safety.[3] In the spring of 1861 Anderson was packed off by steamer to England.

Whether he knew it or not, Anderson had just become a ward of the English followers of William Lloyd Garrison. The Garrisonians, those fervent advocates of immediate abolition, had until recently paid little attention to the Anderson case. The British Garrisonian newspaper, the *Anti-Slavery Advocate*, had merely reprinted excerpts from other abolitionist papers.[4] This may have been because Anderson's cause was under the patronage of men such as John Scoble and Gerrit Smith, notorious anti-Garrisonians. As well, the British agitation in favour of Anderson was led by Chamerovzow and the British and Foreign Anti-Slavery Society, neither of whom conformed to Garrison's orthodoxy. According to the byzantine internal politics of the anti-slavery movement, everyone had to fit within some category. While he was in North America Anderson was associated with the moderate anti-slavery movement; by travelling to England he passed into the custody of the London Emancipation Society, a branch of the Garrisonian faction. Anderson did not appear to have noticed the difference.

The anti-Garrisonians grumbled about the loss of their ward. It was they, after all, who had initiated the mass petition to Newcastle and the legal proceedings. The British and Foreign Anti-Slavery Society cautioned against making Anderson the hero of the hour, and wondered whether he would become 'a charge upon public or private benevolence.'[5] They dissociated themselves from the campaign to promote Anderson: 'We can be no party to his being brought to this country to be lionized.'[6] Officers of the society were conspicuously absent in the ceremonies honouring John Anderson.

The English people seemed mildly surprised by the furore Cockburn's writ had raised on the other side of the Atlantic. The London correspondent of the *Leader* reported that most Englishmen thought that the Canadians would have been glad to get rid of so painful a case.[7] One British newspaper conceded that the English writ had caused great resentment among the Canadians: 'It would have been surprising had it been otherwise. Canada has its courts of appeal, just as we have.'[8] Still, the British were pleased at the outcome and confident that the colonists' ruffled feathers would smooth out over time.

John Anderson arrived in Liverpool in mid-June 1861 and shortly thereafter travelled to London. He was officially welcomed to the city by a huge reception in his honour at Exeter Hall on 2 July. Many speakers, including Harriet Beecher Stowe, had toured England in the anti-slavery cause. Articulate spokesmen for the cause of abolition such as Frederick Douglass and Samuel Ward had spoken throughout the country, giving vivid descriptions of the brutality of slavery and urging the immediate freeing of the slaves. But nothing quite matched the triumphant reception given to the slave who only weeks before had faced the possibility of being returned to the south for a painful death at the hands of slaveowners.

An enthusiastic crowd of more than six thousand packed Exeter Hall to salute John Anderson.[9] On the platform were the members of the newly formed 'John Anderson Committee' and a number of London's prominent clergymen. Sending his regrets was one of England's leading abolitionists, Lord Shaftesbury. The Reverend Harper Twelvetrees, the chairman of the meeting, led Anderson to the podium, where he was received with rapturous applause. After several invocations were recited, Twelvetrees gave Anderson a small bottle of English soil. The label read, 'John Anderson's Certificate of Freedom, presented at Exeter Hall, London, July 2nd, 1861.' He then introduced him to the crowd as 'Citizen Anderson.' After prolonged applause Anderson was called on to speak.

In contrast to speakers such as Douglass and Stowe, Anderson was blunt, almost inarticulate. 'All honour to England,' he began. 'All honour to Her Majesty the Queen for my freedom.' He was almost overcome by the size of the crowd and the emotion of his welcome. He asked to step down, but the audience insisted that he continue. Slowly, Anderson told them of his life in slavery, his killing of Digges, and his flight to Canada. His simplicity and sincerity won over the crowd, and he resumed his seat amid deafening cheers.

Another speaker, the Reverend Cooke Baines, told the people that the purpose of the meeting was to raise money to enable Anderson to get his wife and child out of the south. Maria was not forgotten after all. Perhaps Anderson saw in his sudden notoriety an opportunity to raise the money to buy his family's freedom. If so, it was a daring hope, considering the passage of eight years and the uncertainty prevailing in the United States. Yet despite the enthusiasm that made the Exeter Hall meeting one of the largest anti-slavery gatherings ever held in England, there was still a distinct element of condescension shown towards the blacks. The Reverend Jabez Burns turned towards one of the escaped blacks on the podium, the Reverend Thomas Kinnaird, and ordered him to stand up. Exhibiting the burly Kinnaird to the crowd, Burns declared that he would 'make two Yankees any day. (laughter).' Turning next to Anderson, Burns observed that 'he had an excellent head – in fact, he was altogether a nice looking man.' This was greeted by more laughter. Not only were black objects of amusement, they provided an excuse for some Yankee-bashing. 'The growl of the British Lion went across the Atlantic,' intoned Burns, and struck fear into the hearts of American slave-mongers. England had a right to boast of the 'deep and intense love of liberty' that had made Anderson's freedom possible. At one point Harper Twelve-trees triumphantly saluted 'our happy England – with its free soil, free institutions, and free speech.' Emotions at the meeting seemed to be evenly divided between the humanitarian and the nationalistic.

The great welcome at Exeter Hall also gave English abolitionists a chance to air their views on American secession. A Matthew Fields (possibly a Confederate agent) proposed an amendment to the resolution condemning southern slavery. He suggested that the northern states were as guilty as the southern states in the matter of slavery, and that even if the north prevailed in the conflict slavery would not be abolished. He moved an amendment 'declaring that the black man had more hypocritical and insidious foes to deal with in the men of the Northern States than in the bold man-stealers of the South.' The audience was not fooled. Fields could not get a seconder, and a resolution condemning southern slavery was carried amid much cheering. The Exeter Hall meeting was more proof that English liberal sympathies lay with the northern states. Anderson probably took little note of these amendments and resolutions, but basked in his moment of English glory.

In Anderson the moribund anti-slavery movement had found a symbol to reinvigorate their cause. Moreover, they could join their symbol of spiritual prestige with popular nationalistic sentiments. The meeting at Exeter Hall was only the beginning of a triumphal tour to preach the cause of abolition. Harper Twelvetrees, who was to be the orchestrator of the tour, had treated the crowd to a vivid, and occasionally salacious, description of slavery. 'Deprived by law of the right of marriage,' he intoned, 'the slave was exposed to influences which he should blush to describe in their hearing.' The crowd cheered. With their heavy emphasis on the sadistic and immoral aspects of slavery, the speeches made during Anderson's tour were titillating entertainment as well as serious propaganda.

From Camden Road Chapel to Folkestone, Anderson recited the story of his life and escape from slavery. With each telling the narrative seemed to grow more polished. At Hastings he added considerably more detail to the story of his early life, and described in great flourishes Moses Burton's ineffectual attempts to whip him. On another occasion Anderson added his own compelling description of the slave trade. He had seen slave women sold: 'some of them [were] as white as English women,' but were treated as slaves none the less. 'They are without protection, and white men may do with them as they please.'[10] With his audience's appetite whetted, he continued to recite the story of his escape from slavery.

By October 1861 the committee had decided that Anderson should cease lecturing and acquire some education. Besides, life in London did not suit their charge. These godly clergymen discovered that Anderson had been doing more than giving speeches, and that he had chanced upon 'various influences which, in the metropolis, combined to distract his thoughts and attention.' They delicately declined to describe those influences, but undoubtedly they were not scriptural studies. Anderson was exiled to Corby in Northamptonshire to study at the British Training Institute under the direction of John Pool. For a year, at least, he was safely tucked away in rural England under the eye of the dissenter ministers of the town.

In Canada not everyone had been caught up in the enthusiasm for Anderson. One observer wondered why money was being spent on his education when poor people were going hungry. Perhaps it was the intention of his supporters 'to make a demigod of him.'[11] Another complained that the abolitionists cared nothing for poor whites, but these 'Negro-worshippers' would go into ecstacy over an escaped slave.'[12] These were exceptions, however. For the most part the province rejoiced in Anderson's freedom and hoped that this was the end of the affair. The intricacies of the case were beyond most people, and they did not really care on what basis the court had ordered his freedom. The *London Free Press* probably spoke for most Canadians: 'We profess ourselves to be not at all squeamish. The great object sought, the delivery of Anderson from the hands of his pursuers has been obtained.'[13] American abolitionists also breathed easier now that Anderson was a free man. One of Gerrit Smith's friends wrote to congratulate him for his part in freeing the fugitive. At a time when the American government was making so many concessions to slave power, it was a poor reflection on their republican institutions that 'the monarchical courts have dared to know some *other* law than the law of chattel slavery.'[14]

The end of the legal proceedings did not mean the end of the Anderson case as a political issue. In May 1861 writs were issued for an election and Macdonald's handling of the extradition was sure to be a factor. However, the liberals were in no position to exploit any advantages. George Brown was ill, and his successor, Oliver Mowat, was too inexperienced to be an effective leader. Still, the liberals hoped to exploit Anderson. At the conclusion of the case the *Globe* had warned the public against that oily schemer, John Macdonald: 'Mr Attorney General Macdonald seems to have sustained his political friend Mathews in his kidnapping schemes, and to have declared his opinion at a very early stage in the proceedings, that Anderson was a murderer and ought to be surrendered to the slave-catchers.'[15] In a few ridings, at least, Macdonald's handling of the case was bound to be an election issue.

In Hamilton local reformers tried to coax Samuel Freeman to run against the sitting member, Isaac Buchanan. At a liberal rally speaker after speaker urged Freeman to come forward and accept the challenge. One black man said that he had joined the opposition because he could not forget how Macdonald was willing to betray the fugitives; Freeman had saved 'not only Anderson but every black man in Canada.'[16] Freeman's recent notoriety had made him a likely candidate, and he accepted the nomination reluctantly.

His reluctance was probably due to Buchanan's strength and the government's confidence that he could not be beaten.[17] Buchanan, who had made a fortune in railway speculation, was respected in Hamilton as one of the most adroit businessmen in the province. Although he spoke little in the assembly, and on campaign limited himself to a few Gaelic sayings, the people of Hamilton knew that they had an influential member of the government. Buchanan's supporters at the *Hamilton Spectator* were quick to squelch the *Anderson* case as a source of liberal support. They published Macdonald's letter to Freeman in which the attorney general offered to pay the defence's costs. The *Spectator* artfully omitted Macdonald's statement that in his opinion Anderson was a murderer. Freeman's partisans at the *Hamilton Times* brought this doctoring of the facts to the public's attention, and told the readers that it was Samuel Freeman who had saved the noble Anderson.[18] To the disgust of the *Times*, Hamiltonians voted overwhelmingly for the 'railway chiseller' Buchanan, and rejected Freeman.

Anderson's other defender, John Scoble, was also disappointed. He sought election in West Elgin, but was attacked in the *Toronto Leader* as an 'ex-Chartist' and a 'professional patriot.' The *Chatham Planet* warned the voters that there was something positively revolutionary about Scoble. His 'ultra-demagoguism, over-weening vanity, arrogance and insolence' should disqualify him from office. According to the *Planet*, his abolitionist activities were only a mask for his selfish ambitions. 'The coloured man's interests were made subservient to his own.' Enough of the electors agreed, and Scoble was defeated.[19]

The one place the opposition might profit by attacking Macdonald's handling of the Anderson case was in Toronto. The city was entitled to two members, and the incumbents, George Brown and John Beverley Robinson Jr (son and namesake of the chief justice) had both courted Toronto's black community. During the 1858 celebration of imperial emancipation both members had sent their greetings to the city's black citizens. At the start of the election campaign the younger Robinson had called a special meeting of the black electors of St John's ward and asked for their support. George Brown's *Globe* derided this tactic, and alleged that only a few blacks actually attended the meeting. At another rally on behalf of Robinson's opponent, Adam Wilson, one speaker, W.J. Watkins, savaged Robinson for 'claiming [the blacks'] suffrages, by justifying his father's decision in the Anderson case, which would have sent them all back to slavery.'[20] Using as much exaggeration as he could muster, Watkins tried to portray Robinson as being directly responsible for his father's infamous decision. While it is unknown how well Robinson did among black voters, he was handily re-elected to Parliament. To the great dismay of the reformers, George Brown was defeated. Even in Toronto, where the black vote was so assiduously courted, the ministry's handling of the Anderson affair did not appear to work against the government.

Where the Anderson case and Macdonald's part in it were raised, the opposition candidates went down to defeat. Indeed, Macdonald did well throughout Canada West. Of all of Anderson's defenders, only Matthew Cameron, who ran as a ministerial candidate in the riding of North Ontario, was elected. By the end of the polling the Liberal-Conservative government had gained a majority from both sections of the province, although their majorities in the divided province remained slim. Nevertheless, the attempt to label Macdonald a slave-catcher had completely failed. Protest as the opposition might, the fox had escaped from the trap unharmed and the government had emerged unscathed from a potentially disastrous incident.

Macdonald had not hesitated to use the courts to shield his ministry. As he had declared in St Catharines, Anderson was better off being tried 'by the *Magna Charta*, by the law of the land' than by 'any Cabinet whatever.' This was not saying much for the integrity of Macdonald's cabinet. However, the expedient of using the courts to decide political questions was not new in Canadian politics. In 1852 a reform ministry had referred to the courts the question of an endowment given to the Anglican church. The judges not only dismissed the lawsuit but asked why a question of policy had been brought before them.[21] This use (or misuse) of the judiciary was not unheard of in other British colonies. In the 1820s Australian legislatures had referred a question on the grand jury system to the courts. Judges in two colonies gave conflicting decisions and thereby failed to resolve what the legal adviser of the Colonial Office called 'a matter [more] of general policy than of law.'[22]

Thirty years after the Anderson case, when Macdonald was nearing the end of his career as prime minister of Canada, he found his government threatened by the religious hatreds of the Manitoba school question. The English Protestant majority passed an act in 1890 to eradicate the rights given to French Catholics by the 1870 Manitoba Act. As in the *Anderson* case, Macdonald had an impossible choice. To disallow the act would enrage Protestants, while to uphold it would alienate the French Canadians of Quebec. He therefore permitted a court case to proceed to the Privy Council. The government wished to help the Franco-Manitobans, but as Macdonald's justice minister explained, 'If the appeal should be successful these Acts will be annulled by judicial decision.'[23] In the end, neither the courts nor the government would help the Franco-Manitobans. The *Anderson* case was part of an honoured Canadian tradition of shifting the burden of divisive questions to the courts. If the time required to hear the case did not resolve the question, then, it was hoped, the judges would make a decision and relieve the ministers of unwelcome responsibilities.

Leaving the opprobrium to fall on the judiciary brought no joy to the bench. Without a doubt the *Anderson* case had been a shock to the judicial establishment. The press was outraged that two judges, Robinson and Burns, had decided against freeing the fugitive. To the liberal *Markham Economist*, it was 'truly lamentable that our Courts should be guided by the mere technicalities instead of the spirit of the law they are called upon to explain – It is a disgrace to our age and our country, that people can no longer regard our higher courts as the fountains of justice.'[24] The complexities of the *Anderson* case – the concept of double criminality and the necessity to observe the laws of other states – seemed beyond the comprehension of the public. People looked upon the issue as one of good versus evil, slavery versus freedom, and in that light 'the conduct of the judges looks too like a contemptible evasion of a great public duty.'[25] Nowhere in these devastating condemnations was there any reference to Robinson's having brought the vital *Besset* case to Draper's attention. Nowhere was there any recognition that the Court of Common Pleas had sympathized with the view of the Court of Queen's Bench that habeas corpus was not proper in this case. The issue was one of good versus evil, and Robinson and Burns had shown themselves to be on the side of the latter.

This condemnation was all the more unfair in that the judges had been dragged reluctantly into the affair. At one point Draper had asked Henry Eccles, 'What was the purpose of the Government in sending this case to the Courts instead of deciding it themselves?'[26] The answer was obvious. But it was the duty of the courts to try the case before them, and in so doing to give form and substance to the law. As Philip Kurland has observed, judges determine 'the shape in which a statute is imposed.'[27] In *Anderson* the court gave substance to Article x of the Webster-Ashburton treaty. Even before the signing of the treaty the abolitionists had feared that it could be interpreted to require the extradition of fugitive slaves. In the end, the 'shape of the statute' realized the abolitionists' worst fears. In the opinion of Robinson and Burns, Article x applied to all fugitives, even if their crimes were committed in aid of their escape from slavery. The judges had done their duty as law-interpreters, not as law-makers, and they had created a public resentment that should justly have fallen on the shoulders of John A. Macdonald.

Critics at the time of the Anderson hearing, and later, argued that Robinson's opinion was racially biased and that his belief that blacks were inferior to whites motivated his decision not to quash the warrant of commitment. One of Robinson's antagonists, Charles Durand, observed that 'Judge Robinson's ancestors came from a slave State and the spirit of slavery may have been in him.'[28] Yet there is no indication that Robinson's personal prejudices in any way affected his judicial temperament. In the *Anderson* case he was only applying Article x of the Webster-Ashburton treaty, and he urged the government to use any 'understandings' with the United States on the extradition of fugitive slaves to save Anderson. Thanks to the chief justice, Anderson had been given the benefit of the *Besset* decision and of every possible technical argument in his behalf.

The accusations of racial bias in *Anderson* compare with similar allegations made against Robinson for his decision on separate coloured schools in *Hill* v. *Camden* (1853).[29] In that case the chief justice was asked to set aside the discriminatory requirements of the Common Schools Act (1849), which provided for separate schools for black children in a municipality. Wherever a coloured school had been established, section 12(13) of the act provided that black children could not attend the common or public school. Robinson acknowledged that the provisions had been enacted with some regret by the legislature, to assuage the 'prejudices and ignorance' of some of the white inhabitants. But he must enforce the act, and he concluded that because a separate coloured school existed in the municipality the applicant Hill could not send his children to the common school.

It is inaccurate to conclude that 'this decision in essence sanctioned educational segregation throughout the province. Notwithstanding the intention or spirit of the law, the highest provincial court ruled that black children could be wilfully excluded in virtually any public school district.'[30] The court's decision sanctioned nothing of the kind: it gave effect to a racially discriminatory decision made by the legislature. To argue that the judges should look at the 'intention or spirit of the law' and ignore the plain words of the statute is to misunderstand the role of a British or Canadian judge in the nineteenth century. A judge was to interpret the statutes given to him by Parliament, and he could not read into those statutes his own ideas of what was just. To argue that Robinson could override the words of a statute to allow black children into common schools, or that he could find an exemption for fugitive slaves from the extradition laws, is to ascribe to him an American-style power of constitutional review which he clearly did not possess. The decisions in *Anderson* and *Hill* v. *Camden* do not show racial bias but rather a court determined to apply the law and to leave the political consequences to Parliament.

There is no better way to illustrate the gulf in judicial reasoning between Canadian and American judges of this period than to compare *Anderson* with anti-slavery cases being heard in the United States. American judges frequently reacted to cases concerning slavery by making decisions based on public policy. By the 1840s and 1850s 'lawyers began with frequency to transpose antislavery arguments from political forums into the courts.'[31] For example, in *Prigg* v. *Pennsylvania* (decided in 1842)[32] Justice Story in the u.s. Supreme Court upheld the Fugitive Slave Act of 1793 as vital to the preservation of the Union. Courts gave validity to slave laws because the recognition of those laws was part of the national compact. Other American judges saw slavery as a violation of higher principles of human rights. In *Lemmon* v. *People*(1860)[33] the New

York Court of Appeals refused to apply slave laws outside the south because those laws were contrary to natural right. Decisions based upon public policy were anathema to most Canadian judges. As Queen's Bench (and, to a lesser extent, Common Pleas) had made clear, Anderson would be extradited if the statute so specified. No arguments of political expediency would be allowed to defeat the will of Parliament.

In 1860 extradition treaties were still relatively novel, an outgrowth of the century's innovations in railways and steamship travel. There was a common interest among Western nations in stopping criminals from passing freely from country to country. The *Anderson* case was one of the first attempts by judges to define the limits and powers of extradition. Robinson and Burns had made great efforts to understand the new concept of double criminality. The extradition statute required that the act be a crime not only in the requesting state but in the state in which the accused was being held. But how could a judge determine what was 'murder' when the criminal laws of the two states were dissimilar? Justice Burns thought he had an answer:

Because our laws are different with regard to the liberty of that [slave] class it cannot in reason and common sense be a sound proposition to advance that such difference in the laws warrants us in ignoring altogether the law of the foreign country, and would justify us in saying that a slave cannot commit murder in attempting to escape ... It would be neither fair nor honest to interpret the treaty by the laws of one of the countries, without reference to the laws of the other as they stood at the time the treaty was entered into.[34]

In order to understand the nature of the act – whether it is criminal or not – some recognition must be given to the laws of foreign countries. This reasoning was a significant step in understanding the nature of extradition, and it had the potential to become one of the leading precedents in the field. Initially, however, it was not given that weight.

In 1865 the English Court of Queen's Bench wrestled with the issue of double criminality in the case of *In Re Windsor*.[35] Lawyers for the accused argued that the act (in this case, forgery) had to be a crime in Britain as well as in the requesting state (the United States). They cited Burns J's comment in the *Anderson* case that the evidence of criminality must be such as to justify his commitment for trial in the place where he is found. Justice Blackburn waved off this reference to *Anderson*. 'We came to no decision there beyond this, that, the case being one of life and death, the writ ought to do.' In this breathtaking comment Blackburn revealed that he was unaware that counsel was referring to the Canadian case in which the issue of dual criminality had been thoroughly discussed. He mistakenly referred to the English decision on habeas corpus, a decision that had not touched on the issue. Crown counsel compounded the error. They too dismissed *Anderson*, arguing that 'no question of law was there decided.' The *Anderson* case as a precedent was swept aside by an unthinking bench and uninformed counsel. Cockburn cj held that the criminal act must apply to 'offences which have some common element in the legislation of both countries.'[36] The American definition of forgery would not be recognized in Britain, and the prisoner was released.

In *Re Windsor* became the leading British precedent on extradition. This meant that the Crown had the difficult duty of showing that the crime in the requesting state would also be a crime under English law.[37] The result may have been satisfactory for an island nation, but it created a significant hardship for a country that shared a long, unguarded border with another. English decisions carried great weight in Canada, and *Windsor* was cited again and again as the best explanation of double criminality. The *Anderson* case was cited in a few extradition cases in the late nineteenth century, but mostly on technical points.[38] Canadian judges preferred Westminister's decisions, and applied the high standard for proving double criminality detailed in *In Re Windsor*.[39] With a servility that smacked of colonial times, Canadian judges looked to England for guidance.

Even the leading American text on extradition, published in 1891 by John Bassett Moore, concluded that the rationale in the *Anderson* case had not found acceptance and that the requesting state must show an offence under Canadian law.[40] But Moore's text also referred to the decision of *Re Phipps* (1882)[41] and Hagarty's comments that the court should always lean in favour of sending the fugitive back for trial unless no offence could be made out. John Hagarty (now a chief justice himself) still inclined towards a utilitarian interpretation of the extradition laws. Nevertheless, Moore concluded that the strict interpretation as dictated by *Windsor* prevailed in Canada.

The rationale in the *Anderson* case was resurrected in 1905 by the decision of the British Columbia Supreme Court in *Re Collins*.[42] In that case the accused had committed perjury under California law, and the issue was whether the act was also a crime by Canadian standards. In his decision Justice Lyman Poore Duff placed great reliance on the *Anderson* case. Although it was a case that 'has not been generally followed,' he felt that it was logical to look at the foreign law to determine the substance and essence of the act and then to transfer those facts to Canada to see if the acts would be an offence within the law of Canada: 'It seems to me that in substance the decision of Sir John Beverley Robinson and Mr. Justice Burns is correct in that case, and their decision is an example of the fair and proper application of the provisions in question.'[43] For the same reasons that Robinson and Burns upheld Anderson's warrant of commitment, Duff held that 'no mere deviation from strict ceremonial' could keep perjury committed in California from being perjury in British Columbia. The prisoner was extradited.

By relying on *Anderson* Duff was deliberately evading the principle of *In Re Windsor*. Assisting Duff in the rehabilitation of *Anderson* was a favourable discussion of the case in Sir Edward Clarke's popular *Treatise upon the Law of Extradition*. In a footnote Clarke illustrated his point by citing the English poaching laws. Those game laws might be considered iniquitous in the United States, but a poacher who killed a person who attempted to apprehend him was a murderer, and England would have a legal right to claim him under the treaty. Therefore, the decision of Robinson and Burns that Missouri law must be given some recognition was correct: 'So far as this question was decided in the case of Anderson, it was decided rightly.'[44] Through the intervention of Justice Duff and Sir Edward Clarke, the *Anderson* case was recognized as an important element in Canadian law. Duff's interpretation of double criminality resulted in the extradition treaty's becoming a reliable and not merely an occasional instrument of justice.

The flexible approach defined in *Collins* was affirmed in a number of cases.[45] Moreover, in the twentieth century more and more crimes were being defined by statute. Failure to pay child support, for example, had become a criminal offence in both the United States and Canada. If countries insisted on their own statutory definition of this offence, offenders would easily be able to avoid responsibility. In a Canadian case, *Re Clark* (1929), the presiding judge ruled that even though the law of non-support of minor children was worded differently in the two countries it implied the same offence, and extradition should therefore be granted.[46] In the United States a non-technical interpretation of the extradition statute found an almost universal acceptance. Shiras J held in *Cohn v. Jones* (1900) that 'when an extradition treaty uses general names, such as "murder," "arson," and the like, in defining the classes of crimes for which persons may be extradited, the question of whether a given offence comes within the treaty must be determined by the law as it exists in the two countries at the time the extradition is applied for.'[47] The intent of the court in this case is almost identical with that of Robinson and Burns in *Anderson*. The U.S. Supreme Court in *Wright* v. *Henkel* (1903) also endorsed the utilitarian view of extradition treaties; Chief Justice Fuller held that 'treaties must receive a fair interpretation, according to the intention of the contracting parties.'[48] One writer has observed that Canadian and American courts are quick to see 'kindred offences.' An American judge in *Perez Jimenez* (1960) considered the diversion of funds in Venezuela to be the equivalent of embezzlement in the United States.[49] Likewise, in *Ex Parte Pendergast* (1968) a charge of grand larceny laid in New York was found to be similar to the Canadian offence of obtaining money under false pretences.[50] As a result, 'the reciprocal experience of Canada and the United States as neighboring states has done much to insure the satisfactory reliance of this interpretative approach to double criminality.'[51]

In Britain, however, controversy over the nature of double criminality continued to plague the bench and provide employment for barristers. The tendency persisted in Britain to evaluate crimes by British standards. A royal commission concluded in 1878 that 'our own law will afford a sufficient test [for ascertaining an offence] being abundantly comprehensive as to offences against person and property.'[52] This rigid position was consistently applied after *Windsor*. In *King* v. *Dix* (1902) an English court would not permit extradition on a charge of larceny because American law was not in conformity with English requirements for the elements of the offence.[53] It was not until the *Budlong* case (1980) that the English Court of Queen's Bench held that so long as crimes were 'substantially similar' in both countries extradition should follow.[54] The House of Lords in *Re Neilson* (1984) denounced this approach, however, and insisted that it is 'English law alone that is relevant.'[55]

For Canada, at least, the *Anderson* case eventually was recognized as a useful precedent. In the 1977 edition of the text *Extradition to and from Canada*, G.V. LaForest concluded that 'The approach taken in *Re Anderson* seems to be the only logical one; the institutions and laws of the foreign country must necessarily form the background against which to examine events occurring in that country. It is, after all, the essence of the offence that is important in extradition.'[56]

Praise from twentieth-century jurists was poor consolation for Robinson and Burns. By the nature of their office they were compelled to suffer in silence while the *Globe* sneered at the defective law and weak logic of their un-British decision.'[57] In their only correspondence during this period, the chief justice and the attorney general discussed the application of the criminal law and the state of the prisons without mentioning the Anderson controversy. This was proper, for it would have been a breach of ethics for them to discuss a case that was still pending before the courts. One of the few journals to speak up for the judges was the *Hamilton Spectator*. Whether or not one agreed with the judges, the *Spectator* said, they should be honoured for having followed their honest convictions.[58] Perhaps the most eloquent defence of the Canadian judges was a comment not published in Canada. The English *Law Times* pointed out that neither Robinson nor Burns had ruled in favour of slavery. They had taken a difficult statute and tried to make sense of it: 'These judges, proof against unpopularity, and unswayed by their own bitter hatred of slavery, as well as unsoftened by their feeling for a fellow-man in agonising peril, would uphold the law made to their hands, and which they are sworn faithfully to administer. *Fait justicia*. Give them their due: such men are the ballast of nations.'[59]

If the *Anderson* case embarrassed the judiciary, it shocked the politicians. To their dismay they discovered just how lightly their rights were regarded in Britain. Since the implementation of responsible government in the 1840s Canadians had created their own sovereign institutions. They had thought that their prerogatives would be respected by Britain. The Montreal newspaper *Le Canadien* (which had supported Anderson) summed up the colonial dismay: 'Mais les colonies ayant une législature à elles doivent par égard pour leur dignité, et encore plus pour prévenir de dangereux conflits d'autorité, insister sur leur droit à une juridiction exclusive dans tous les autres cas.' Not only should Canadians stand on their rights, they should expect the mother country to foster the process of nation-building. By interfering with the authority of the Canadian judges the English judiciary had lowered the status of their Canadian counterparts.[60] Were Canadian institutions now liable to be set aside at a British whim? The English writ of habeas corpus was a rebuke that must be answered.

The answer was to come from John A. Macdonald. Although Macdonald is often remembered as an unbending advocate of the imperial connection, the *Anderson* case revealed his sensitivity to imperial interference in Canadian affairs. In a letter to the governor general Macdonald tried to explain the urgency of the matter. A fundamental question was at stake, which 'is justly considered here as directly affecting the independence of our Courts and our people. The province had its own courts, he reminded the governor general, and the exercise of legal writs in Canada by English courts would almost certainly 'produce an unseemly and irritating conflict of Jurisdiction.' The only solution was for the British Parliament to pass an act in the next session abolishing the rights of English courts to issue writs in Canada.[61] A few days later, on 16 March 1861, Macdonald used the throne speech at the opening of the legislature to publicize his confrontation with Westminster. Her Majesty's government in Canada advised the British government of 'the expediency of preventing by legislation in Great Britain any possible conflict in jurisdiction.'[62] The colonists were now telling the mother country which acts to pass!

The ensuing debate showed the ministry and the opposition to be arguing at cross-purposes. Macdonald wanted to debate this threat to Canadian nationhood; the liberals were more interested in rehashing the past sins of the government. John Sandfield Macdonald, who had largely inherited the opposition leadership after Brown's defeat, jumped on the ministry's lack of 'pluck' in shifting the responsibility for the case onto the courts. The attorney general tried to remind him that it was the fugitive's own lawyer who had sued for habeas corpus. This was the last chance for the liberals to make political capital out of the case, and Oliver Mowat spoke passionately about how the ministry had been foiled in its attempt to deliver Anderson up to the slave-catchers. Asking the British to change their laws was not enough, Mowat maintained, Canada should amend its own Fugitive Offenders' Act to take the power of committal away from justices of the peace.[63]

Stealing the opposition's thunder, Macdonald moved on 2 April to amend the Fugitive Offenders' Act. In addition to stripping the justices of the peace of their authority, the amendments made a significant change in the wording. Under the previous act, evience had to be sufficient only 'to sustain the charge according to the laws of this Province.' The amended section required evidence that 'would justify the apprehension and committal for trial of the person so accused.' Now the evidence had to do more than merely sustain the charge; it had to be sufficient actually to commit the accused to trail. Under this higher standard it might have been difficult for Anderson (and genuine criminals) to be returned to justice. The Lower Canadian *rouge*, A.A. Dorion, wanted further guarantees that extradited persons would get fair trials. Wearily, Macdonald explained that the source of their authority was the Webster-Ashburton treaty, which did not envisage giving the extraditing state this kind of power.[64] The opposition grumbled, but the new act was made law and sanctioned by Queen Victoria.

Canadians had put their own house in order. Now they looked to Britain to see how she would deal with this threat to colonial self-government. Ever since responsible government had been conceded to the British American colonies in the mid-1840s the exact nature of the system had eluded statesmen. It was established practice for the governor to choose his ministers from the faction that could control the legislature and to give the ministers control of patronage appointments. During the controversy over the Canadian government's determination to pay damages to suspected rebels, among others, by the Rebellion Losses Bill (1849), British conservatives made common cause with colonial conservatives in opposing this measure.[65] Despite its dislike of the bill, the British government supported the right of the Canadian legislature to enact it. This was 'the only true parliamentary test responsible goverment ever achieved,'[66] and a vindication of the rights of the Canadian legislature. The Australian colonies also had been granted responsible government. In this new age the Colonial Office 'was to yield to almost every thrust of Australian self-assertion.'[67] Still, colonial self-government remained an undefined concept. True to the unwritten British constitution, it was formed by circumstances and incidents, not by some definitive statement. One permanent undersecretary of the Colonial Office haltingly tried to explain the system: '"Responsible Government" in this country [New Zealand] rests on no law, but simply on recognized usage ... it [is] not established by any law.'[68]

In two important ways the *Anderson* case elaborated on the breadth and width of colonial self-government. In external affairs the British government continued to exercise unquestioned authority. London's instruction to the governor general not to release Anderson was not resented in Canada; Haliburton railed against the act in Westminster, but in the province it went largely without comment. On the one hand, Canadians still respected the right of Britain to act for them in international affairs. As recent as 1854 Britain had negotiated the crucial reciprocity treaty with the United States for Canada's benefit. If British officials of the Foreign Office wished to consider the Anderson case and its effect on the Webster-Ashburton treaty, Canadians could have no cause for complaint. On the other hand, there was furious resentment of the British courts' issuing a writ in Canada. By 1860 Canadians looked upon their courts as being supreme in the province, subject, of course, to the final right of appeal to the Privy Council in London.[69] In the daily routine of judicial affairs, Canadian judges were expected to be masters in their own houses. George Macbeth observed in the Canadian assembly, 'It is evident that the exercise of this jurisdiction is utterly inconsistent with the principles of local self-government on which our constitution and our relations with the mother-country are based.'[70]

The mother country agreed. In March 1862 the British government introduced a bill to prevent writs of habeas corpus from being issued to Canada. In introducing the bill the colonial undersecretary, Chichester-Fortescue, admitted that 'it arose out of the case of the fugitive slave Anderson' and was intended to prevent the recurrence of such an intrusion. The only opposition to the bill was based on a fear that it might prevent appeals to the Privy Council. The attorney general assured the House that that fear was groundless, and the bill was quickly passed into law.[71] British reaction to the colonists' outrage over the English writ was proof that responsible government provided the empire with a graceful means of withdrawal from confrontations with the colonies. The Anderson case was a minor incident in this 'gradual relaxation of ties ... as a prelude to the grant of independence'[72] and a sign of Britain's willingness to let the Canadians control their own courts and domestic affairs.

The *Anderson* case had become one of those incidents that gave substance to the policy of imperial disengagement. The ease with which the British government acknowledged the inviolability of provincial institutions was an indication of the flexibility of imperial control. While Britain retained control over extraterritorial matters, the Colonial Office was astute enough to realize that colonial courts and legislatures should be given a free hand. The colonial officers acted to ensure that a case like Anderson's would never again ruffle Canadian feelings. It was this sensitivity to colonial self-government that was to maintain the harmonious relationship between the mother country and the emerging nations of the empire. It was no small accomplishment.

10

Back to Africa

John Anderson's odyssey ended in Africa. After a year at the British Training Institute at Corby, Anderson had learned how to read, write, and do simple mathematics. He had testimonials from the local clergy on his piety and sobriety. Now that they had succeeded in turning him into a proper Englishman, the members of the Committee for John Anderson wondered what they should do with their charge. None of these gentlemen, apparently, ever contemplated that he might want to make his own way in the world. F.W. Chesson of the London Emancipation Society suggested that he be sent to the free black republic of Liberia. The society enthusiastically seized upon his idea, and together with Gerald Ralston, the Liberian consul general in England, arrangements were made for Anderson to go to Africa. Ralston arranged for letters of introduction to the principal officers of state in Liberia, and Chesson solicited the African Mail Company for a free passage to West Africa. Ralston wrote that Anderson would be sure to succeed in Liberia, for 'there is the greatest abundance of natural wealth in Liberia; and only capital and skilled labour are required to develop it.'[1]

A farewell soirée was held in Anderson's honour in London on 22 December 1862. Chesson had arranged for a free grant of land in Liberia and passage (second class) on a steamer. Now the Committee for John Anderson could indulge in self-congratulation. At the dinner one of the leading black figures in London, Professor W.G. Allen, gave a short lecture on the opportunities available in Liberia. Recounting the glorious history of old Africa, he expressed his certainty that Liberia would surpass the achievements of Egypt and Ethiopia. When he was in America, Allen, like most blacks, had shared the 'strong prejudice' against emigration to Liberia. It was widely felt that the 'back to Africa' movement was intended by evil-minded whites as a way of exiling former slaves. Almost all freed blacks felt that they had as much right to remain in America as whites. But over the years Allen had changed his mind; he now looked upon Liberia, 'this green and inviting spot,' as a future paradise for black settlers, a place where ambition and industry could create a nation rivalling America in prosperity. To the amusement of the guests, Allen added that if it had not been for his wife's strong objections he would have left for Liberia long ago. F.W. Chesson also spoke of Liberia's tremendous potential. Chesson had once met Liberia's President Stephen Allen Benson, and he was impressed by the erudition of the African-educated statesman. Almost as an afterthought the committee members called on John Anderson to speak. He admitted that, like Professor Allen, he had once 'felt a great prejudice against Liberia – against even the very name of it,' but from what he now knew about the country he was willing to make (or reconciled to making) his future there.

A few days after the dinner the committee members escorted Anderson to Euston Station. From there he travelled to Liverpool where he met John Pool, who safely saw him on board a packet. Now that he had served his purpose as a symbol of the struggle against slavery, the abolitionists seemed eager to ensure that he was quickly shipped out of England. On 24 December 1862 John Anderson set sail on the *Armenian*, bound for Cape Palmas, Liberia.

Anderson probably disembarked at Cape Palmas early in 1863. Repatriated slaves had formed a commonwealth in this part of west Africa in 1822, and in 1847 they declared an independent republic. However, the settlers, the Americo-Liberians, had received little support and no diplomatic recognition from the United States. In addition, they lived in continual fear of the encroachments of the imperial powers, France and Britain. Disease, the threat of attack from hostile tribes in the interior, and torrential rainfall had not made Liberia a prosperous nation. There is no record of John Anderson's leaving any descendants in the Cape Palmas area. It is possible that he emigrated eastwards to the British colony of the Gold Coast. The colony received aid from Britain, and the authorities could have used a trained craftsman like Anderson to build their fortifications. Or Anderson might have migrated north to Liberia's capital, Monrovia, where he might have become part of the Americo-Liberian establishment.[2]

Or did he return to Africa at all? Many years later, an American naval officer, Uriel S. Sebree of Fayette, Missouri, spoke with a black American at a European port. The black man asked Sebree about Missouri and specifically about the Digges killing. Sebree remembered the incident, but when he tried to pursue this mysterious individual, the man disappeared. Sebree was convinced that he had stumbled upon Seneca Digges's killer.[3] Did Anderson jump ship before reaching Liberia, or did he become disenchanted with Liberia and return to Europe? His remarks at his farewell soirée showed that he was not enthusiastic about going to West Africa. His final destination after his departure from Liverpool in 1862 remains a mystery.

Back in Missouri, thousands of miles from Liberia, the Digges family had given up hope of ever seeing John Anderson put on trial. Seneca Digges had been buried on his farm; his grave can no longer be located. His sons continued to farm in Howard County, and Benjamin Digges's great-grandson Dale Richardson lives there today. Over the years the story of the killing of Seneca Digges passed into local lore, but the facts became blurred and exaggerated. No record remains of Maria or of Anderson's child. Samuel Brown, Maria's owner, was killed during the slavery agitation just before the outbreak of the civil war. His property, including his slaves, was sold off.[4]

In Canada interest in Anderson's fate dissipated as quickly as it had arisen. Perhaps only the active abolitionists remembered or cared about the case. At its annual meeting in February 1863 the Anti-Slavery Society of Canada congratulated itself on having rescued Anderson: 'He is now a freeman, occupying a good position in the free Republic of Liberia, instead of having suffered a felon's doom under circumstances of the greatest barbarity.'[5] The *Anderson* case had come upon the public and politicians like a thunderclap, and had departed as quickly. The incident was mentioned in the British parliament's inquiry into the extradition laws, but it did not affect the inquiry.[6] By the end of the legal proceedings all attention was fixed on the American Civil War, and Anderson faded from memory.

Newspapers were filled with accounts of battle and the effect of the war on North America. While Canadians such as George Brown rallied to the cause of north and the emancipation of the slaves, others feared a reunited and expanionist United States. After the Civil War Brown and Macdonald would bury their enmity and work together to create a nation capable of resisting incorporation into the United States. Both John Scoble and Matthew Cameron would sit in Parliament during the Confederation debates and play a small role in the creation of the Dominion of Canada in

1867. By the 1860s the prerogative of Canadians to create and use their own institutions was beyond challenge. During the Confederation debates of 1865 George Brown declared, 'A revolution has occurred in Great Britain on the subject of colonial relations to the parent state.'[7] The *Anderson* case was a small but telling skirmish in that revolution. It was proof of the British withdrawal from the affairs of the self-reliant colonies.

John A. Macdonald became the new nation's first prime minister in 1867. He remained in office, except for one defeat during the Pacific Scandal, until his death in 1891. George Brown left politics after Confederation and devoted himself to his *Globe* and his businesses. He was still regarded as one of the great men of Canada when he was murdered by a disgruntled employee in 1880.

As for Anderson's defence lawyers, Samuel Freeman achieved a quiet eminence in Hamilton. In 1865 there were rumours that he might be apppointed to Queen's Bench, but nothing came of it and he had to be satisfied with elevation to the modest post of clerk of the peace. He died in 1874. Matthew Crooks Cameron pursued his admirable but lonely course in politics. Elected to Parliament a number of times, he became the leader of the Conservative opposition in Ontario in 1871. When the Liberal government introduced a resolution stating that no effectual steps had been taken to bring to justice the murderers of the Orangeman Thomas Scott, Cameron, alone among the entire membership of the House, voted against the motion. Criminal acts were to be judged by the courts, not by the legislature, he declared. In recognition of his independence and integrity he was made a justice of the Court of Queen's Bench in 1878.[8]

Anderson's English defender, Edwin James, was not fated to prosper. His tendency to mislead others caught up with him shortly after the Anderson hearing. In April 1861 he was forced to declare bankruptcy, and criminal investigators charged him with fraud. In July he was disbarred, and fled in disgrace to New York.[9]

Only two years after these events, in November 1863, Henry Eccles died in Toronto. His partner in the Crown prosecution, Robert A. Harrison, went on to a spectacular career in the Ontario legal profession. His textbooks were read throughout the Anglo-American world, and his skill in a courtroom was undeniable. In 1875, at the age of forty-two, he became chief justice of Ontario. His time on the bench was short, however; he died three years later.[10]

If any group lost prestige as a result of the *Anderson* case, it was the province's judiciary. They had suffered silently while individuals such as

Professor Daniel Wilson had proclaimed that 'there are cases, and this is one of them, in which we feel that an appeal lies beyond the mere technical definition of the law.'[11] It must have been frustrating to hear calls for them to do things which, as British judges, they were specifically forbidden to do. They had to apply the law; they could not release Anderson merely because the *Globe* editorialists considered him to be innocent. To change the law to protect fugitive slaves was the prerogative of politicians such as Macdonald and Brown, not of jurists such as Robinson and Burns.

Sir John Beverley Robinson retired from the bench in January 1862. He had been ill for many years, and there is no indication that his retirement was hastened by the Anderson controversy. At the time of Robinson's death, in January 1863 (when Anderson would have been first setting foot in Liberia), unpleasant memories of the case were still apparent. His obituary noted that as a result of the case 'so strongly prejudiced was public opinion that the popularity of the bench seemed likely to suffer.'[12] But Robinson had done his duty, and his decisions, including his decision in the Anderson case, would provide a wealth of useful opinions for succeeding generations.

Archibald McLean succeeded Sir John Beverley Robinson as chief justice in 1862. At the time of his death in 1865 he was widely praised for his decision in the *Anderson* case. 'Whatever may be the strict law of the case,' said the *Upper Canada Law Journal*, 'one cannot help admiring the free British spirit so characteristic of the man.'[13] Praise in an obituary was to be expected. But the question remained: was it the province of a judge to apply his own sense of 'free spirit' to the acts of Parliament?

During its brief notoriety the *Anderson* case provoked a great public outcry against slavery. It showed that most Canadians were eager to protect the fugitives and the underground railroad. Massive public pressure was brought on the courts on Anderson's behalf, and appeals were made to 'higher' or 'natural' notions of law. To the defence's disappointment, these arguments were rejected; the final decision was a triumph of the technical over the spiritual. Yet the outcome was testimony to the strength of the rule of law in Canada. The decision of Robinson and Burns was a fair application of the law enacted by Parliament. In the tradition of British justice they had given an objective interpretation of the law in the face of an outraged public. Well they deserved the praise of the English *Law Times*: '*Fiat justicia*. Give them their due. Such men are the ballast of nations.'

Notes

1 IN LITTLE DIXIE

1 Details of Anderson's youth are contained in Harper Twelvetrees (ed.) *The Story of the Life of John Anderson, The Fugitive Slave* (1863; reprint, Freeport, NY: The Black Heritage Library Collection 1971) 8–10 and 128–9.

2 Paul C. Nagel *Missouri: A Bicentennial History* (New York: Norton 1977) 75

3 Perry McCandless *A History of Missouri, 1820–1860* vol. 2 (Columbia: University of Missouri Press 1972) 60

4 Joint Collection, University of Missouri Western Historical Manuscript Collection and Columbia and State Historical Society of Missouri Manuscripts (hereinafter Missouri manuscripts) collection no. 49, North Todd Gentry 'Missouri Laws and Proceedings Concerning Slavery,' address to the Boone County Historical Society (n.d.); see also McCandless *History* 57–8.

5 Robert W. Fogel and Stanley L. Engerman *Time on the Cross: The Economics of American Negro Slavery* vol. 1 (Boston: Little, Brown 1974) 147

6 Twelvetrees *John Anderson* 128–9

7 McCandless *History* vol. 2, 58. Free blacks could not live in Missouri unless they possessed a licence from the county court. They could not testify at the trial of a white man, and they could not hold an assembly without a white official present.

8 Twelvetrees *John Anderson* 131–2

9 Kenneth M. Stampp *The Peculiar Institution: Slavery in the Ante-Bellum South* (New York: Knopf 1965) 185

10 Twelvetrees *John Anderson* 129–30

2 A SUDDEN IMPULSE

1 Reported in the *Glasgow Times* 1 December 1853
2 Ibid. 25 August 1853
3 2 September 1853
4 *Glasgow Times* 2 July 1853
5 Ibid. 20 October 1853
6 Ibid. 22 December 1853
7 Revised Statutes of Missouri 1845
8 *In the Matter of John Anderson* (1860) 20 UCQBR 126–33
9 Twelvetrees *John Anderson* 16
10 *Toronto Leader* 26 November 1860, 'Petition of John Anderson.' Anderson's petition, presented to the justice of the peace at Brantford, is not reported in 20 UCQBR.
11 *Toronto Leader* 26 November 1860
12 Twelvetrees *John Anderson* 16–17
13 *Glasgow Times* 6 October 1853
14 Ibid. 27 October 1853
15 The story of Anderson's escape and flight to Canada is given in Twelvetrees *John Anderson* 17–20
16 *Glasgow Times* 13 October 1853
17 Georgina M. Falls *The Local History of the Windsor Border Region* vol. 5 (Windsor 1970) 3
18 Laura S. Haviland *A Woman's Life-work: Labors and Experiences* (Chicago 1887) 197–205
19 *Glasgow Times* 27 October 1853
20 *Liberty Tribune* 9 December 1853. The Missouri newspaper reported an incident in which a Kentucky man was lashed by the slave he was pursuing. The Canadian authorities made no attempt to arrest any of the blacks involved in the incident. In an editorial comment the *Tribune* added, 'The day may come when some of the countless indignities committed by the black-hearted and craven "negro stealers" who border the lakes, may be appropriately repaid.'
21 *Detroit Daily Advertiser* 14 September 1860
22 Gerrit Smith Collection, Syracuse University (hereinafter Gerrit Smith Collection), Haviland to Smith, 21 February 1861
23 Haviland *A Woman's Life-work* 206–7

3 MAGISTRATE MATHEWS'S PRISONER

1 Sandwich *Voice of the Fugitive* 12 March 1851
2 Joan Magee *Loyalist Mosaic: A Multi-ethnic Heritage* (Toronto: Dundurn Press 1984) 90–1
3 Quoted in Robin W. Winks *The Blacks in Canada: A History* (New Haven: Yale University Press 1977) 149
4 Arthur to Sydenham, 15 October 1840; reprinted in Charles R. Sanderson (ed.) *The Arthur Papers; Being the Canadian Papers Mainly Confidential, Private and Demi-official of Sir George Arthur, KCH* (Toronto: University of Toronto Press and Toronto Public Libraries 1959) 149–50
5 *Sandwich and Amherstburg Maple Leaf* 16 July 1857, reprinted in R.A. Douglas *John Prince 1796–1870: A Collection of Documents* (Toronto: Champlain Society 1980) 156
6 Winks *The Blacks* 251
7 Patrick Brode *Sir John Beverley Robinson: Bone and Sinew of the Compact* (Toronto: The Osgoode Society 1984) 265
8 Ontario Archives, Upper Canada Sundries, vol. 40, 18673–4, Robinson to Maitland, 8 July 1818
9 See Jason H. Silverman *Unwelcome Guests: Canada West's Response to American Fugitive Slaves, 1800–1865* (Millwood: Associated Faculty Press 1985).
10 Winks *The Blacks* 246–7
11 Fred Landon 'The Anti-Slavery Society of Canada' *Ontario History* 48 (1956) 125, and I.C. Pemberton '*The Anti-Slavery Society of Canada*' MA thesis (University of Toronto 1967)
12 3 Will. IV, c.7 (UC)
13 J.M. Leask 'Jesse Happy: A Fugitive Slave from Kentucky' *Ontario History* 54 (1962) 87, at 98
14 Ibid. 95
15 Alexander L. Murray 'The Extradition of Fugitive Slaves from Canada: A Re-evaluation' *Canadian Historical Review* 43 (1962) 298, at 300
16 Murray 'Extradition' 314. The durability of the erroneous idea that dual criminality protected fugitive slaves is shown by its repetition: see Winks *The Blacks* 172 and Silverman *Unwelcome Guests* 41–2.
17 Governor General Bagot to Colonial Secretary Lord Stanley, 20 January 1842, reprinted in *British Parliamentary Papers – Area Studies – United States of America – Correspondence and Other Papers relating to Fugitive Criminals and the Slave Trade* vol. 46 (Shannon: Irish University Press 1971) at 9 (hereinafter *British Parliamentary Papers USA*)

18 Ashburton to Webster, 7 August 1842 *British Parliamentary Papers USA* vol. 12, 40
19 David M. Turley ' "Free Air" and Fugitive Slaves: British Abolitionists versus Government over American Fugitives 1834–61' in Christine Bolt and Seymour Drescher (eds) *Anti-Slavery, Religion, and Reform: Essays in Memory of Roger Anstey* (Folkstone: Wm Dawson 1980) 163–82
20 Murray 'Extradition' 302
21 British Museum, Aberdeen Papers, Aberdeen to Ashburton, 26 May 1842; reprinted in W.D. Jones 'The Influence of Slavery on the Webster-Ashburton Negotiations' *Journal of Southern History* 22 (1956) 48, at 50
22 Murray 'Extradition' 309
23 *Hansard Parliamentary Debates* 3d ser., vol. 70 (30 June 1843) col. 472
24 Judges to Lieutenant-Governor Cockburn (n.d.) *British Parliamentary Papers USA* vol. 46, 27
25 Secretary of State John C. Calhoun to the American minister in London: reprinted in Manley O. Hudson 'The Factor Case and Double Criminality in Extradition' *American Journal of International Law* 28 (1934) 274, at 298
26 Ashburton to Clarkson, 17 March 1843; reprinted in A.H. Abel and F.J. Klingberg (eds) *A Side-light on Anglo-American Relations, 1839–1858 Furnished by the Correspondence of Lewis Tappan and Others with the British and Foreign Anti-Slavery Society* (1927; reprinted New York: Kelley 1970) 33
27 *Grand River Sachem* 11 April 1860
28 *Hamilton Daily Spectator* 5 December 1860 (W. Mathews's letter to the editor, 3 December 1860). See also *Toronto News of the Week* 5 April 1860: 'It appears that the charge was preferred by a fellow colored man, who came with him into Canada shortly after the murder.'
29 *Toronto Globe* 29 November 1860. John Scoble informed a crowd in Toronto that 'Mathews the magistrate ... had meanwhile sent to Detroit and procured a man named Gunning to swear an information against Anderson': *Toronto Globe* 20 December 1860
30 *Brantford Expositor* 6 April 1860
31 *Hamilton Daily Spectator* 5 December 1860
32 *Toronto Globe* 9 April 1860
33 Abel and Klingberg *Side-light* 125
34 R.D. Webb to Elizabeth Pease, 4 November 1840; reprinted in Howard Temperley *British Antislavery 1833–1870* (London: Longman 1972) at 210. See also Winks *The Blacks* 201–4.
35 *Detroit Daily Advertiser* 14 September 1860
36 *Norfolk Messenger*; quoted in the *London Free Press* 5 October 1860
37 *Hamilton Daily Spectator* 5 December 1860

38 *Toronto Leader* 7 February 1859. Justice McLean, in admonishing the kidnappers, remarked, 'We know that parties committing crimes have been frequently abducted not only from our own country but from the States.'
39 *Toronto Globe* 14 November 1860
40 *Hamilton Daily Spectator* 14 December 1860
41 *Toronto Globe* 18 February 1860

4   A CAUSE CÉLÈBRE

1 Charles M. Johnston *Brant County: A History 1784–1945* (Toronto: Oxford University Press 1967) 30
2 *Brantford Expositor* 20 May 1859
3 Ibid. 7 January 1859
4 Johnston *Brant County* 38
5 *Toronto Globe* 9 January 1857
6 *Brantford Expositor* 12 August 1859
7 Ibid. 3 August 1860
8 *In the Matter of John Anderson* (1860) 20 UCQBR 124, at 127
9 Ibid. 128
10 Ibid. 129
11 Ibid. 130
12 *Toronto Globe* 1 March 1861
13 *Toronto Leader* 26 November 1860
14 *Brantford Expositor* 5 October 1860
15 *Toronto Globe* 23 November 1857
16 Ontario Archives, George Brown Papers, ms. 91, McGee to Brown, 1 October 1860
17 J.M.S. Careless *Brown of the Globe: The Voice of Upper Canada 1818–1859* (Toronto: Macmillan 1959) 314–22
18 Province of Canada, no. 22 in *Sessional Papers* (1861) vol. 4, Macdonald to Freeman, 18 October 1860
19 Ibid., Freeman to Macdonald, 6 October 1860
20 *Toronto Globe* 14 November 1860
21 Donald Creighton *John A. Macdonald: The Young Politician* (Toronto: Macmillan 1952) 297
22 Issues of the *Hamilton Times* for this period are not extant. See the *Brantford Expositor* of 5 October 1860: 'Our Confrere of the Hamilton *Times*, usually so cool, and so discreet in the discussion of public topics, seems to have become perfectly rabid, on the arrest of the negro Anderson, alias Jack Burton, on the charge of murder; and without waiting to hear the evidence

advanced in support of the charge, endeavors to forestall public opinion, by abusing in merciless terms every officer who had anything to do with the arrest of the criminal.'

23 *Hamilton Times*, quoted in *Toronto Globe* 14 November 1860
24 *Toronto Globe* 28 November 1860
25 *Toronto Leader* 11 and 28 January 1859
26 24 December 1860
27 Ontario Archives, George Brown Papers, ms. 91, Mowat to Brown, 15 December 1859
28 Russell to Head, 27 October 1860 *British Parliamentary Papers USA* vol. 46, 118
29 Cass to Irvine, 2 November 1860 *British Parliamentary Papers USA* vol. 46, 163
30 Newcastle Papers, University of Nottingham Library, Newcastle to Head, 5 June 1861
31 *Toronto Globe* 25 September 1860
32 *Detroit Daily Advertiser* 14 September 1860
33 Ibid. 15 Septembr 1860
34 *Baltimore American* 3 December 1860
35 *Toronto Globe* 12 February 1861
36 *New York Times* 30 January 1861
37 *Sarnia Observer* 28 December 1860

5 ARGUMENT AND PLEADING

1 *Journal of Education for Ontario* no. 27 (Toronto: 1874) 91
2 *Woodstock Sentinel*, quoted in *Hamilton Daily Spectator* 27 October 1860
3 *Toronto Globe* 21 October 1859
4 *Chatham Planet* 3 December 1860
5 J.C. Dent *The Canadian Portrait Gallery* vol. 3 (Toronto: 1881) 89
6 *Simcoe News*, quoted in *Kingston Daily British Whig* 26 November 1860
7 *Toronto Globe* 30 November 1860 and *Toronto Leader* 30 November 1860
8 Daniel G. Hill 'Negroes in Toronto, 1793–1865' *Ontario History* 55 (1963) 73–91
9 J.M.S. Careless *Toronto to 1918: An Illustrated History* (Toronto: Lorimer 1984) 73–4
10 *Toronto Leader* 24 November 1860
11 *In the Matter of John Anderson* (1860) 20 UCQBR 134
12 *Toronto Leader* 26 November 1860. Portions of the legal argument that are recorded in the *Leader* do not appear in the published case.
13 Supra note 11, 136–7
14 Ibid. 138
15 Daniel J. Boorstin *The Mysterious Science of the Law* (Cambridge: Harvard University Press 1958) 158

16 Supra note 11, 140
17 Ibid. 143–4
18 Ibid. 144, 147
19 4 *Taunt.* 34, 128 ER. 239 (1811)
20 *Russell on Crimes* vol. 1, 7th U.S. ed., 535
21 Supra note 11, 148
22 Ibid. 149
23 *Toronto Leader* 26 November 1860
24 *Simcoe News*, quoted in *Kingston Daily Whig* 26 November 1860
25 *Toronto Globe* 28 November 1860
26 *Toronto Leader* 24 November 1860
27 *Ottawa Citizen* 4 December 1860
28 *Norfolk Messenger* 8 November 1860
29 *Toronto Leader* 15 December 1860
30 Ibid. 30 November 1860
31 *Toronto Globe* 30 November 1860
32 Ibid. 10 December and 3 December 1860
33 Ibid. 3 December 1860
34 Ibid. 5 December 1860
35 *Mirror of Parliament* Legislative Council, 3 April 1860, no. 3, Hon. Col. Prince:
   'Great doubts existed at present in the minds of the magistrates, especially
   on the frontiers, as to the manner in which the treaty, under the conflicting
   statutes, was to be carried out' (at 3).
36 23 Vict., c. 41 (Can.)
37 *Toronto Globe* 11 December 1860
38 Ibid. 9 May 1860
39 *Toronto Leader* 21 December 1860. Harrison's letter was eventually printed in
   the *Globe* on 24 December 1860.
40 *Durham Standard* 4 January 1861
41 Ontario Archives, George Brown Papers, McGee to Clark, 10 December 1860
42 *Norfolk Messenger* 8 November 1860
43 *Toronto Globe* 10 December 1860
44 *Brantford Expositor* 26 October 1860
45 *Hamilton Daily Spectator* 16 November and 14 December 1860
46 Quoted in J.K. Johnson 'John A. Macdonald' in J.M.S. Careless (ed.) *The
   Pre-Confederation Premiers: Ontario Government Leaders, 1841–1867* (Toronto:
   Ontario Historical Studies Series 1980) 209
47 Quoted in *Chatham Planet* 10 December 1860 (emphasis in original)
48 *London Free Press* 14 December 1860
49 *Brantford Expositor* 2 November 1860
50 *Toronto Globe* 5 December 1860

51 Ibid. 8 December 1860
52 *New York Times* 29 November 1860
53 *Toronto Globe* 24 January 1861
54 Ibid. 7 January 1861. In the end, the u.s. Supreme Court ruled that Governor Dennison was wrong in ignoring the validity of slave laws in extradition cases. See F. Simkin 'The Strange Career of Fugivity in the History of Interstate Extradition' *Utah Law Review* (1984) 511, at 514.
55 *Toronto Globe* 9 January 1861
56 *Detroit Daily Advertiser* 25 December 1860
57 *New York Daily Tribune* 29 November 1860; reprinted in the *Chicago Tribune* 4 December 1860
58 The editorial in the *New York Tribune* of 29 November 1860 was reprinted in the *Boston Liberator* on 31 December 1860. This was one of the few comments in the *Liberator* on the Anderson case.
59 *Memphis Daily Appeal* 30 January 1861
60 *Baltimore American* 3 December 1860
61 *New York Times* 29 November 1860

6 'THE WRANGLING COURTS AND STUBBORN LAW'

1 J.E. Farewell 'The Anderson Case' *Canadian Law Times* 32 (1912) 256, at 258
2 Of the judges of Queen's Bench appointed after 1829, Robinson, McLean, Jonas Jones, and James Macaulay had all studied at Cornwall Grammar School. Robinson and McLean had fought together at Queenston Heights, and two of their fellow judges, Macaulay and Christopher Hagerman, had distinguished military service. In the political era after the War of 1812 Robinson, McLean, Jones, and Hagerman had all been prominent tory leaders.
3 9 December 1845
4 30 January 1847
5 *Toronto Globe* 24 April 1857
6 *Toronto Leader* 8 December 1860
7 Ibid. 14 February 1859
8 Careless *Brown* 263–80
9 *Toronto Globe* 20 December 1858. Of the three lawsuits, *Macdonell* v. *Macdonald* was argued in Common Pleas and *Macdonell* v. *Smith* and *Macdonell* v. *VanKoughnett* in Queen's Bench.
10 *Toronto Leader* 10 December 1860
11 *Toronto Globe* 17 December 1860
12 Farewell 'The Anderson Case' 260
13 *In the Matter of John Anderson* (1860) 20 UCQBR 124, at 162

14 The Webster-Ashburton treaty had been put into effect in Great Britain by
   1843, 6 & 7 Vict., c. 76. However, it was not convenient to apply the
   British statute in Canada: see 1 *Moore on Extradition* 627. Section 5 of the
   imperial act gave power to the province to pass its own enabling act;
   therefore the Canadian act of 1849, 12 Vict., c. 19, replaced 6 & 7 Vict., c. 76
   and enacted the Webster-Ashburton treaty in the province.

15 Supra note 13, 168–9 (emphasis in original)

16 Ibid. 172

17 Ibid. 173

18 Ibid. 186–8

19 Ibid. 190

20 Compare Burns J's decision with Roman J. Zorn 'Criminal Extradition
   Menaces the Canadian Haven for Fugitive Slaves, 1841–1861' *Canadian
   Historical Review* 37 (1957) 284: 'It was abolitionist agitation that induced
   Britain to exclude slaves from extradition under the Webster-Ashburton
   Treaty' (294).

21 Supra note 13, 191–2

22 *Chatham Planet* 19 December 1860

23 *Perth Courier* 11 January 1861 and Sarnia *Observer* 28 December 1860

24 *Brockville Recorder* 27 December 1860

25 *Perth Courier* 15 February 1861

16 *Toronto Globe* 18 December 1860

27 *Montreal Pilot* 17 December 1860

28 *Hamilton Daily Spectator* 17 December 1860

29 *Saint John News*, quoted in the *Toronto Globe* 26 January 1861

30 *Toronto Globe* 20 December 1860

31 Ibid. 26 December 1860

32 Ibid. 4 January 1861 and *Hamilton Daily Spectator* 4 January 1861

33 *Le Canadien* (Montreal) 3, 12, and 21 December 1860

34 *La Minerve* (Montreal) 2 February 1861

35 *Quebec Mercury* quoted in the *Toronto Globe* 25 December 1860

36 *Montreal Pilot* 17 December 1860

37 *Quebec Mercury*, as quoted in the *Toronto Globe* 25 December 1860

38 *Toronto Globe* 16 January 1861

7 ENGLAND INTERVENES

 1 Bodleian Library, Oxford University, Anti-Slavery Papers (hereinafter Anti-
   Slavery Papers), Henning to Chamerovzow, 17 December 1860. See also
   R.C. Reinders 'Anglo-Canadian Abolitionism: The John Anderson Case,

1860–1861' *Renaissance and Modern Studies* 19 (1975) 72, at 78. This article, along with R.C. Reinders 'The John Anderson Case, 1860–1861: A Study in Anglo-Canadian Imperial Relations' *Canadian Historical Review* 56 (1975) 393, gives a thorough account of the attempts made by British abolitionists to secure John Anderson's freedom.

2 Howard Temperley *British Antislavery 1833–1870* (London: Longman 1972) chapter 10. See also C. Peter Ripley (ed.) *The Black Abolitionist Papers: The British Isles 1830–1865* (Chapel Hill: University of North Carolina Press 1985) 3–5

3 On Louis Alexis Chamerovzow, see Ripley *Abolitionist Papers* 384.

4 Reinders 'Anglo-Canadian Abolitionism' 82

5 *Punch* 12 January 1861

6 *Liverpool Mercury* 17 January 1861 and *London Post*; as quoted in the *Toronto Globe* 22 January 1861

7 *Glasgow North British Daily Mail* 16 January 1861; *Economist* 12 January 1861; and *London Dial* 4 January 1861

8 Leeds *Mercury* 5 January 1861: 'We confess that we are reluctantly obliged to adopt the opinion of the majority of the Court.' See also *London Times* 5 January 1861.

9 *London Despatch* 29 December 1860

10 Province of Canada, no. 22 in *Sessional Papers* (1861) vol. 4, Newcastle to Williams, 9 January 1861

11 Public Records Office, Russell Papers, folio 93, Russell to Newcastle, 9 January 1861. This letter was brought to my attention by Dr Ged Martin.

12 Reinders 'Anglo-Canadian Abolitionism' 84

13 *Anti-Slavery Papers* (minutes of the British and Foreign Anti-Slavery Society) 14 January 1861

14 Sir William Holdsworth *A History of English Law* vol. 15, edited by A.L. Goodhart and H.G. Hanbury (London: Methuen 1965) 431–2

15 The details of James's life can be found in *Dictionary of National Biography* vol. 10 (Oxford 1921–22).

16 Proceedings before the English court of Queen's Bench are reported in the *Law Times* of 19 January 1861, 622–4, and 3 El. & El. 487; 121 E.R. 525 and in the shorthand notes prepared at the instigation of the American legation in London and printed in *United States Senate Executive Documents* serial 1082, vol. 4, doc. 11, 18–44 (hereinafter *Executive Documents*).

17 *Law Times* 19 January 1861, 622

18 See *Leith* v. *Willis* (1836) 5 UCQB (O.S.) 101. Robinson CJ ruled that the English Gin Acts of the early eighteenth century were of no relevance and therefore of no effect in Canada: 'The main scope of the statute is for purposes wholly foreign to us' (103).

19 *Executive Documents* 23–4
20 *Law Times* 19 January 1861, 623
21 *Executive Documents* 34–6
22 31 Geo. III, c. 31, s. 34
23 34 George III, c. 2 (UC)
24 *Executive Documents* 36
25 Ibid. 41
26 *Law Times* 19 January 1861, 624
27 *London Times* 16 January 1861
28 *London Morning Star* 16 January 1861; *Liverpool Mercury* 17 January 1861; and *London Standard* 17 January 1861
29 *London Times* 16 January 1861
30 *Toronto Globe* 13 February 1861 (London correspondent)
31 *Law Times* 12 January 1861, 125
32 *London Times* 16 January 1861
33 *Law Times* 19 January 1861, 139
34 *The Jurist* 7 (n.s., pt. 2) 23 February 1861, 73
35 *Law Magazine* 11 (1861) 42, at 48
36 Ibid. 46: Habeas Corpus Act, 1678, 31 Car. II. c 2. The writ ran to England, Wales, Jersey, and Guernsey. The act was amended in 1816 by 56 Geo. III, c. 100, to extend jurisdiction to the Isle of Man.
37 4 T. R., 503, 100 ER 143 (1792). An action in trespass would not lie in the courts at Westminster for entering a house in Canada.
38 *The Jurist* 7 (n.s., pt. 2) 9 February 1861, 43–5
39 Reinders 'The John Anderson Case' 407, quoting *Journal of Jurisprudence* 5 February 1861, 83–5
40 1 B. & S. 400, at 410–11; 121 ER 764, at 770
41 *R.* v. *Earl of Crewe, Ex Parte Sekgome* [1910] 2 KB 576; 26 TLR 439
42 *Ex Parte Mwenya* [1960] 1 QB 241, [1959] 3 WLR 509 (DC): [1959] 3 WLR 767, [1959] 3 All ER 525 (CA) at 293 (QB)
43 *In Re Keenan* [1972] 1 QB 533, at 542
44 *Liverpool Post* 17 January 1861, as quoted in the *Toronto Globe* 2 February 1861
45 Peter Burroughs 'Colonial Self-Government' in C.C. Eldridge (ed.) *British Imperialism in the Nineteenth Century* (New York: St Martin's Press 1984) 39, at 61
46 *Law Times* 19 January 1861, 138
47 Head to Stanley, 11 June 1858, quoted in D.G.G. Kerr *Sir Edmund Head: A Scholarly Governor* (Toronto: University of Toronto Press 1954) 207
48 *The North British Review* 33 (1860) 51
49 *Hansard Parliamentary Debates* 3d ser., vol. 161 (8 February 1861) H.B. Sheridan (col. 219), Mr Warner (col. 221)

50 Ibid. Viscount Palmerston (col. 224)
51 Ibid., T.C. Haliburton, 22 February 1861 (cols. 822–825)
52 Ibid. Chichester-Fortescue (col. 827)
53 O.W. Hewett *'And Mr Fortescue': A Selection from the Diaries from 1851 to 1862 of Chichester Fortescue, by Lord Carlingford, KP* (London 1958) 179

8 A CASE OF QUIBBLES

1 Dallas to Black, 16 January 1861 *Executive Documents* 4
2 As quoted in David M. Potter *The Impending Crisis 1848–1861* (New York: Harper and Row 1976) 563
3 30 January 1861: 'Were we under a state of less painful excitement at home, this case would command an extraordinary degree of attention in this country.'
4 30 January 1861
5 See the *New York Herald* 2 February, 7 February, and 17 February 1861.
6 *Buffalo Republic*, quoted in the *Hamilton Weekly Spectator* 7 February 1861
7 Anti-Slavery Papers, Henning to Chamerovzow, 17 December 1860
8 *Memphis Daily Appeal* 30 January 1861
9 Gerrit Smith Collection, Scoble to Smith, 4 January 1861
10 *Toronto Globe* 19 January 1861
11 Gerrit Smith Collection, Angelina Grimké Weld to Smith, 30 January 1861; and see H. Catlin to Smith, 20 February 1861, and J.B. Sanborn to Smith, 29 January 1861.
12 Brian Jenkins *Britain and the War for the Union* vol. 1 (Montreal: McGill-Queen's University Press 1974) 2–5
13 *Charleston Daily Courier* 19 December and 29 January 1861; *Washington Daily National Intelligencer* 30 January 1861; and *New York Herald* 23 December 1860
14 30 January 1861
15 William N. Brigance *Jeremiah Sullivan Black: A Defender of the Constitution and the Ten Commandments* (Philadelphia 1934; reprinted New York 1971): 'All business of the administration was centered upon the crisis of Secession. The problem of foreign affairs was very much in the background' (111). See also U.S. Senate *Congressional Globe* 11 February 1861, 841
16 *Montreal Gazette* 2 February 1861
17 2 February 1861
18 8 February 1861. See also *Markham Economist* 7 February 1861: 'Such interference with the independent jurisdiction of our Canadian Courts should not be permitted in any account.'

19 *Hamilton Weekly Spectator* 31 January 1861
20 *Montreal Advertiser* 6 February 1861
21 31 January 1861
22 *Toronto Globe* 8 February 1861
23 (March 1861) 53
24 *Law Times* Queen's Bench, 19 January 1861, 620–2. The discussion of the origins of the Canadian courts appears only in the u.s. Senate *Executive Documents*.
25 7 February 1861
26 Province of Canada, no. 22 in *Sessional Papers* (1861) vol. 4, Paterson and Harrison to Deputy Attorney General H. Bernard, 11 December 1860
27 Ibid. Freeman to Macdonald, 18 December 1860. 'I have the strongest hope that I shall be able to relieve you from the necessity of making an order for the surrender of "the negro."'
28 Ibid. Freeman to Macdonald 24 December 1860
29 *Toronto Globe* 2 February 1861
30 Freeman to Macdonald, 22 October 1861 (the date is in error; the correct date is probably 2 February 1861) *Sessional Papers supra note 26*
31 *Toronto Globe* 11 February 1861
32 See George Metcalf 'William Henry Draper' in J.M.S. Careless (ed.) *The Pre-Confederation Premiers: Ontario Government Leaders, 1841–1867* (Toronto: Ontario Historical Studies Series 1980). For example, Draper had put forward a rate bill that would have required all property owners to contribute to school taxes. This bill was bitterly opposed by the tory faction.
33 Ontario Archives, Miscellaneous Collection, Brown to Richards, 8 March 1844. Brown asked Richards for political articles, particularly 'anything spicey.'
34 Metropolitan Toronto Library, pamphlet collection, John Hawkins Hagarty *Thoughts on Law Reform* (1845)
35 *Toronto Globe* 9 January 1857
36 *Toronto Leader* 7 January 1859
37 The extracts from the Court of Common Pleas are taken from two sources – the official report, *In Re John Anderson (1861) 11 uccp 1*, and the *Toronto Globe* 11 February 1861.
38 11 uccp 23–4
39 Ibid. 26–9
40 *Toronto Globe* 11 February 1861
41 Ibid.
42 Ibid.
43 11 uccp 39–40

44 *Toronto Globe* 11 February 1861
45 1732, 5 Geo. II, c. 7, *An act for the more easy recovery of debts in his Majesty's plantations and colonies in America.* The statute enabled English creditors to sell a debtor's negroes to satisfy a debt.
46 *Toronto Globe* 11 February 1861
47 Ibid.
48 Ibid.
49 3 Zabriskie 311–21 (1857)
50 11 UCCP 47
51 *Toronto Globe* 11 February 1861
52 J.K. Johnson and Carole B. Stelmack *The Papers of the Prime Ministers: The Letters of Sir John A. Macdonald 1858–1861* (Ottawa: Public Archives of Canada 1969), Macdonald to the provincial secretary, 17 January 1861, concerning the extradition case of Joseph Bocarde: 'The copy of the evidence as certified by the Magistrate in this case is not alone sufficient. The papers should therefore be returned to Mr Matthews, the Magistrate that he may certify as required by chap. 89 of the Consolidated Statutes of Canada sect. 1, that the evidence is deemed sufficient by him to sustain the charge according to the laws of this Province if the offence alleged had been committed herein, together with the copy of the testimony' (204)
53 12 February 1861
54 *Sarnia Observer* 15 February 1861
55 Henning had served the writ on the Toronto sheriff so that in the event of an adverse decision Sheriff Jarvis would be obliged to send Anderson to England. See Gerrit Smith Collection, Henning to Smith, 13 February 1861. Jarvis replied, 'I am not instructed to make any formal return to the Writ of Habeas Corpus.' Anti-Slavery Papers, Jarvis to Henning, 16 February 1861.
56 *Toronto Leader* 15 February 1861
57 11 UCCP 54
58 (1844) 6 QB 481; 115 ER 180
59 Ibid. 60
60 Ibid. 71
61 *Toronto Globe* 18 February 1861
62 *Hamilton Daily Spectator* 18 February 1861
63 *Quebec Chronicle*, quoted in the *Ottawa Citizen* 22 February 1861
64 *Brockville Weekly Recorder* 7 February 1861
65 19 February 1861
66 *Grand River Sachem* 20 February 1861
67 *London Free Press* 18 February 1861
68 Freeman to Macdonald, 18 February 1861 *Sessional Papers supra note 26*

9 'TO MAKE A DEMIGOD OF HIM'

1 *Hamilton Weekly Spectator* 18 February 1861
2 Ibid. 28 February 1861
3 Gerrit Smith Collection, Freeman to Smith, 18 February 1861
4 Reinders 'Anglo-Canadian Abolitionism' 92
5 *Anti-Slavery Reporter* 1 May 1861, and Anti-Slavery Papers, minutes of the British and Foreign Anti-Slavery Society, 5 April 1861: 'But the Committee were unanimously of opinion that no encouragement to visit England should be held out to [Anderson].'
6 *Anti-Slavery Reporter* 1 July 1861
7 *Toronto Leader* 12 March 1861
8 *Willmer & Smith's Times* 2 March 1861, quoted in the *Toronto Globe* 20 March 1861
9 Twelvetrees *John Anderson* 86–124
10 Ibid. 128–9
11 *Toronto Leader* 1 March 1861
12 *Norfolk Messenger* 4 April 1861
13 18 February 1861
14 Gerrit Smith Collection, H. Catlin to Smith, 20 February 1861
15 19 February 1861
16 *Hamilton Times* 17 June 1861
17 *Toronto Leader* 20 June 1861
18 *Hamilton Times* 20 June 1861
19 *Chatham Planet* 6 June 1861; Scoble contested the victory by the government candidate, George MacBeth, and in another election held on 23 February 1863 Scoble was elected.
20 *Toronto Globe* 2 July 1861
21 *Attorney General* v. *Grasset* (1856) 5 Gr. 412. Chancellor Blake: 'If it be true that this grant is objectionable ... that is matter proper for the Legislature, with which as a court of justice, we have no concern' (432–3).
22 Stephen to Hay, 1 April 1826, quoted in Alex C. Castles 'The Judiciary and Political Questions: The First Australian Experience, 1824–1825' *Adelaide Law Rev.* 5 (1975) 294, at 312
23 Report to Council by Sir John Thompson, minister of justice, 21 March 1891, quoted in Lovell C. Clark (ed.) *The Manitoba School Question: Majority Rule or Minority Rights?* (Toronto: Copp Clark 1968) 127
24 28 February 1861
25 *Montreal Gazette* 18 February 1861
26 *Toronto Globe* 11 February 1861

27 Philip B. Kurland *Politics, the Constitution, and the Warren Court* (Chicago: University of Chicago Press 1970) 69

28 Charles Durand *Reminiscences of Charles Durand of Toronto, Barrister* (Toronto: Hunter Rose 1897) 444

29 (1853) 11 UCQBR 573. See also H.W. Arthurs 'Civil Liberties – Public Schools – Segregation of Negro Students' *Canadian Bar Review* 41 (1963) 453.

30 Jason H. Silverman and Donna J. Gillie 'The Pursuit of Knowledge under Difficulties': Education and the Fugitive Slave in Canada' *Ontario History* 74 (1982) 95, at 102

31 William E. Nelson 'The Impact of the Antislavery Movement Upon Styles of Judicial Reasoning in Nineteenth Century America' *Harvard Law Review* 87 (January 1974) 513, at 525

32 41 US (16 Pet.) 539

33 20 NY 562

34 (1860) 20 UCQBR 124, at 191–2

35 (1865) 6 B. & S. 522; 122 ER 1288

36 Ibid. 528 (B.&S.) 1291 (ER)

37 This principle was to be repeated in English cases. See *Re Bellencontre* [1891] 2 QB 122: 'The person whose extradition is sought should have been accused in a foreign country of something which is a crime by English law, and ... there should be a prima facie case made out that he is guilty of a crime under foreign law, and also of a crime under English law' (per Willis J).

38 *In Re Warner* (1864) 1 UCLJ (n.s.) 16, and *In Re Burly* (1865) 1 UCLJ (n.s.) 20

39 *Re Hall* (1882) 9 Ont. PR 373; *Re Smith* (1868) 4 Ont. PR 215; *Ex Parte Lamirande* (1866) 10 LC Jr. 280

40 J.B. Moore *A Treatise on Extradition and Interstate Rendition* (Boston: Boston Book Company 1891) 647–8

41 (1882) 1 OR 586

42 (No. 3) (1905) 10 CCC 80

43 Ibid. 102

44 Sir Edward Clarke *A Treatise Upon the Law of Extradition* (London: Stevens and Haynes 1874) 187

45 *State of Washington* v. *Fletcher* (No. 2) [1926] 2 WWR 508; *Re Brooks* (1930) 66 OLR 158; *State of New York* v. *Kaslov* (1950) 97 CCC 146; *Ex parte O'Dell and Griffen* [1953] OR 190; *Re Whipple* [1972] 2 WWR 613

46 [1929] 3 DLR 737, at 748

47 100 Fed. 639, at 645 (1900)

48 190 U.S. 40, at 58 (1903)

49 177 F. Supp. 856 (1959)

50 (1968) 6 Crim. LQ 394

51 M. Cherif Bassiouni *International Extradition and World Public Order* (New York: Oceana 1974) 343–4
52 As quoted in Hudson 'The Factor Case' 282
53 (1902) 18 TLR 231
54 *Governor of Pentonville Prison, ex parte Budlong* [1980] 1 WLR 1110: 'It cannot have been intended that this foreign warrant should set out all the ingredients of the English offence … Such an oppressive requirement would, of course, make extradition unworkable' (Griffiths J at 1115).
55 *Re Neilson* [1984] AC 606: 'I can find no justification whatever in the act of 1870 for adducing at the hearing before the magistrate, under sections 9 and 10, evidence of foreign law … at the conclusion of the evidence the magistrate must decide whether such evidence would, *as according to the law of England*, justify the committal for trial' (at 624, per Lord Diplock; emphasis in original).
56 G.V. LaForest *Extradition to and from Canada* 2d ed. (Toronto: Canada Law Book 1977) 53
57 27 February 1861
58 18 February 1861
59 12 January 1861 128
60 *Le Canadien* (Montreal) 6 February 1861
61 Province of Canada, no. 22 in Sessional Papers (1861) vol. 4, Macdonald to Sir Edmund Head, 6 March 1861
62 *Morning Chronicle's Parliamentary Debates* 4th Sess., 6th Parlt, Province of Canada, 16 March 1861
63 Ibid. 20 March 1861
64 Ibid. 1 May 1861
65 Ged Martin 'The Canadian Rebellion Losses Bill of 1849 in British Politics' *Journal of Imperial and Commonwealth History* 6 (1977) 3
66 John W. Cell *British Colonial Administration in the Mid-Nineteenth Century: The Policy-Making Process* (New Haven: Yale University Press 1970) 116
67 Charles S. Blackton 'The Cannon Street Episode: An Aspect of Anglo-Australian Relations' *Historical Studies* 13 (1969) 520, at 532. In the colonies of Victoria and New South Wales there continued to be claims of imperial interference in domestic affairs: see Geoffrey Serle 'New Light on the Colonial Office, Sir George Brown, and the Victorian Constitutional Crises' *Historical Studies* 13 (1969) 533.
68 Merivale to Wynyard, 10 August 1854, quoted in Cell *British Colonial Administration* 142
69 During the same session that the amendment to the Fugitive Offenders' Act was debated, a member proposed abolishing the right of appeal to the

Privy Council. One legislative councillor replied that 'as long as he lived under the British flag, he hoped he should never be deprived of the right of appeal to the highest court of the Empire.' Supra note 62, 17 May 1861.
70 Ibid. 18 March 1861
71 *Hansard Parliamentary Debates* 3d ser., vol. 166 (1862) cols. 328–329
72 C.C. Eldridge *England's Mission: The Imperial Idea in the Age of Gladstone and Disraeli 1868–1880* (Chapel Hill: University of North Carolina Press 1973) 37

10   BACK TO AFRICA

1 Twelvetrees *John Anderson* 152
2 J.G. Liebenow *Liberia: The Evolution of Privilege* (Ithaca: Cornell University Press 1969). I wish to thank Mr George Anderson (no relation to John Anderson) of Cape Palmas, Liberia, for his help in discussing the Cape Palmas area and Liberian history.
3 Letter from J.P. Howard of Fayette, Missouri (1989) enclosing a newspaper clipping of a 1923 Fayette, Missouri, centennial newspaper. Reported under the heading 'Killed by a Runaway Slave.'
4 *History of Chariton and Howard Counties* (1923) 560. I wish to thank Dale Richardson and Mrs Charles Coutts of Fayette, Missouri, for their information on Howard County.
5 *Toronto Globe* 5 February 1863
6 *Report of the Select Committee of the House of Commons on Extradition* 6 July 1868, 3–4. In 1881 memories of *Anderson* were fresh enough that the case figured prominently in J.C. Dent's *The Last Forty Years: Canada Since the Union of 1841* (Toronto: George Virtue) 404–6. J.E. Farewell's reminiscence of the case appeared in *Canadian Law Times* 32 (1912) at 256. However, the incident faded into obscurity, and in W.L. Morton's 1964 study of the Union of British North America for the Canadian Centenary Series, Anderson's case is mentioned only briefly (and innacurately) in a footnote: 'In the matter of the extradition of Anderson, an escaped American slave, the British Court of Common Pleas had overruled the Canadian courts.' See W.L. Morton *The Critical Years: The Union of British North America 1857–1873* (Toronto: McClelland and Stewart) 90. In Brian Jenkins's 1974 study of Anglo-American relations during the Civil War, the *Anderson* case is not mentioned: see Brian Jenkins *British and the War for the Union* (Montreal: McGill-Queen's University Press). Interest in *Anderson* was revived by Robert C. Reinders's two articles on the case which appeared in 1975 (see note 1, chapter 7, supra).

7 *Parliamentary Debates on Confederation* 3d Sess., 8th Parlt, Province of Canada, 8 February 1865, 97
8 Samuel B. Freeman *Journal of Education for Ontario* vol. 27 (1874) 91. For Cameron see J.C. Dent *The Canadian Portrait Gallery* vol. 3 (Toronto 1881) 100.
9 *Dictionary of National Biography* vol. 10 (1921–22)
10 Henry Eccles (obituary) *Toronto Globe* 3 November 1863. For Robert A. Harrison see Dent *Canadian Portrait Gallery* vol. 3, 89.
11 *Toronto Globe* 20 December 1860
12 *Upper Canada Law Journal* (March 1863) 63
13 Ibid., new series vol. 1 (November 1865) 282

Index